Endorsements

I cried reading through the stories in An Awareness of Grace *because of the realization that great faith doesn't come from us, it comes from a strong foundation and commitment to Jesus Christ.*

JULIE RICHARDSON
ENTREPRENEUR/BUSINESS OWNER

This book was riveting. It kept me on the edge as I turned each page. This story of God's grace is so believable even if you don't know the author. This book of experiences is one for this age and the ages to come. Debbie has an uncanny way of bringing you alongside her in the story.
She has a creative way with words to help even the young, as well as older reader, understand and yearn for this experience of God's amazing grace.
Debbie, I am honored to publicly applaud you as you continue in your very apparent literary gifts.
Thanks for sharing your experiences with us.

WYVONNEA ALLEN
PASTOR AND BUSINESS OWNER

I've had the privilege of knowing Debbie for almost two decades. She has always lived out and been ready to share her stories and answers to prayer always bringing glory to a powerful and loving God. Debbie held onto her faith even during trying times. God always showed Himself faithful. My prayer is as people read this book they will be inspired to live a life glorifying God.

CATHERINE MIJARES
FOURSQUARE PASTOR

An Awareness of Grace *is rich with awesome miracles. It is full of love, compassion, patience, humor, and faith.* An Awareness of Grace *reminds me that we serve a mighty God who never fails us.... He daily blesses us with miracles. I love how Debbie Powers incorporates Scripture to every chapter and how it comes alive in her journey, but also in ours if we heed to it. Debbie Powers's stories move you from believing what God says to receiving what He gives in so many unexpected ways, but always gloriously wonderful. God is still the God of miracles, and Debbie clearly and beautifully expressed that in every chapter! This book walks you into the throne of God by the many miracles of God Debbie shared and lived.... It truly is "an awareness of grace."*

AIDA MEACHAM
ORDAINED SENIOR PASTOR AND CHURCH PLANTER

A testimony is a powerful thing! In her book, An Awareness of Grace, *Debbie Powers shares story after story of God's grace and goodness in her life. With a sweet vulnerability she unfolds the narrative of God's healing, grace, and peace during the storms of life. If you doubt that God can do the impossible, read this book. If your faith is weak and needs to be strengthened, read this book. If you need to find Jesus, read this book. His fingerprints are all over it.*

SUSIE STARR
ORDAINED MINISTER WITH ASSEMBLIES OF GOD,
KIDS MINISTRY, EVANGELIST, VENTRILOQUIST.
PERFORMING ARTS INSTRUCTOR

Debbie writes with excitement as she shares her faith through her stories of God's grace. I love the way she tells her stories, with such passion, such authenticity, and even some humor that breaks the tension when needed. I highly recommend reading this book. It will boost your faith and encourage your prayer life.

SUSAN MONTGOMERY
DISTRICT LICENSED MINISTER OF THE CHURCH OF
THE NAZARENE, ASSOCIATE PASTOR AT VALLEY VIEW
CHURCH OF THE NAZARENE IN LANCASTER, CA

I have known Debbie for several years and one thing I love about her is she does not wear her struggles on her sleeve. While she may appear to be the definition of carefree, she's not. She's careful to let God care for her. Because of this, she has a powerful testimony to share.
She's dazzled us all over the years with her unique talents, joy, and artistic methods of showing God's love for us all. As she is now embarking upon the journey of writing her stories for us all, I know this book will be well worth the read, and the reread.

HILARY SMART
CHRISTIAN MINISTRY LEADER
WIFE AND MOTHER

Debbie's gift of storytelling took me from smiling to laughing to crying from one chapter to the next as I was reminded of God's faithfulness in my own life. This delightful collection of real-life stories will encourage you to keep your heart and eyes open to see God at work in your everyday life too. Definitely a "good for the soul" read.

REV. DR. SANDY WEINBERG
HOSPICE CHAPLAIN

an AWARENESS

of Grace

Stories of Divine Intervention in Daily Life

DEBBIE POWERS

Dedication

This book is dedicated to the Father, Son, and Holy Spirit who have been with me throughout my life and encouraged me to write and share my testimony.

Contents

Acknowledgments

I want to thank my awesome family: Jack, my husband (RIP), and Jessie, Nikki, and Jacquee, my beautiful daughters, for allowing me to share our life in the pages of *An Awareness of Grace* and being part of the journey that this book is all about. You are my blessings and my heart. I love you so much.

I am eternally grateful for Pastor Aida Meacham who encouraged me years ago to write my book. She always believed in me and pushed me out of my comfort zone. Then she cheered me on when I started writing. I couldn't ask for a truer friend.

A special thanks to Pastor Catherine Mijares, who mentored me as I grew in my faith and for her love and patience as I grew under her leadership.

This book would not have happened if it wasn't for my publisher, HigherLife Publishing, who took on my book and believed it was worthy of publishing. Especially my project manager, Virginia Grounds, who walked me through every step with gentle encouragement and understanding. I can't tell you how many times she calmed my nerves and helped me move forward.

I'm so grateful for my church family. When they heard about my book, they prayed and encouraged me on my journey to be published.

I want to thank the following awe-inspiring folks who believed in me and financially gave to my funding campaign so I could publish. Your monetary support blessed me and confirmed that this is what God wanted me to do. I pray God blesses you a hundredfold: Don MacArthur, Steve Seward, Russel Di Bernando, Stewart Cain, Barbara Beals, Julie Richardson, Silvana Rivas, Dolores Coleman, Jeannie Pero, Kari Bianco, Karen Roy, Denise Coffield, Pastor John and Aimee Aartman, Angeline Vallmer, and Nancy Arreseigor. And to all the others who gave after the final edit, I have not forgotten you. You are in my prayers to be blessed for your generous support.

Preface

The stories in this book are about a loving God who interacts with His creation. This is my personal witness of how God has worked in my life. As you read these stories, I pray you will realize God's desire for an intimate relationship with you too. The purpose of *An Awareness of Grace* is to boast about my loving God, my Abba Father.

> *Oh, give thanks to the Lord; call upon his name; make known his deeds among the peoples! Sing to him, sing praises to him; tell of all his wondrous works!*
> (Psalm 105:1–2 ESV)

There are three kinds of people you will encounter when you share your testimony:

- Those who weren't there, so they don't believe you.
- Those who believe that *you* believe it happened, but it was probably a coincidence.
- Those who believe and want to share your story because they were encouraged by it.

As you read my testimony, I hope and pray it will encourage you into a deeper relationship with the Lord. Since you weren't there to see these things firsthand, you might find some of the stories hard to believe. You might think I'm making more of these experiences than is warranted.

However, there are people who will recognize God's Spirit in my journey and long for more of God in their lives. I hope that is you.

The stories are in no particular order, but each one has its own unique theme. The same golden thread is woven throughout each, which is God's provision.

Chapter 1

As for God, his way is perfect: the Lord's word is flawless;
He shields all who take refuge in him.
(PSALM 18:30)

Miracle of 1994

Was that a scream?

I lost focus on the telephone conversation with my sister, as I stretched the phone cord as far as it would go to peer outside. I couldn't see anything. Probably a boy chasing a girl. Yea, that's what it was. No need to look.

Seconds later, the door flew open. Four young people screamed, "Call 9-1-1. Call 9-1-1."

*****

Earlier that day…

Why did I do this to myself? Am I a glutton for punishment? The night was going to be hectic, but I couldn't get out of it now even if I wanted to. What made it worse was, I couldn't sit back in the carpool and take a nap or at least rest a little. Boy, I could have used it too. I'd been up since four that morning.

Unfortunately, it was my turn to drive. I wished I had remembered that when I committed to cooking for the Youth's Christmas Caroling/Progressive Dinner outing. It would have been so much easier if I agreed to do a dessert or salad. But no. I signed up to cook the main dish.

It was 3:45 p.m., and the workday was done, but my day was far from over. Punctuality was the name of the game now, and I hoped everyone would get off work on time so our carpool could get on the road.

I sensed an urgency in my spirit. I hated running late and feared I wouldn't have enough time to prepare.

Our commute was usually long, slow, and nerve-racking. It would take an hour or more to drive the fifty miles to where I would drop off my passengers and another twenty miles until I reached my home.

My mission was to get home by five o'clock, 5:30 at the latest, and start cooking two tons of spaghetti. Well, maybe not quite that much.

The church youth planned to bundle up and ride on a hay wagon for an old-time effect as they went from house to house. Surely, I would have plenty of time to get home and be ready by 6:30 when everyone would arrive. In the meantime, Pastor Rob planned to pick up my three daughters at five o'clock and take them to the church where they would meet forty other kids and chaperones.

I was punctual for the carpool, but unfortunately, nobody else was. Of all times, there was an accident on the freeway. So much for being home by 5:30 at the latest.

It was after 6:30 when I sped into the driveway, threw my vehicle into park, jumped out, and ran into the house. I threw my purse and coat on the table, grabbed the biggest pot I had, filled it with water, and put it on the stove to boil.

Time to get myself ready and make a yuletide atmosphere for the crowd that would soon be arriving. My mind worked overtime. I hoped they'd call before coming over. They had started at 5:30 and had to go eat salad at the first house in the progressive dinner. Then there was the bread house.

Oh, no! I realized it couldn't possibly take very long for those two stops. Maybe they would stay longer at the house where the salad would be served and sing for a while.

My heart pounded. Would I be ready when they showed up? Why was the water taking forever to boil? I tried not to watch it.

Should I make meat sauce or sauce with meatballs? How I wished I had planned better. I decided to make some of each.

The sauce looked great, but if the water didn't boil soon, I would have nothing to put it on.

Why did I do this to myself? I was wound up like a spring and had nobody to vent to.

Finally, the spaghetti was in the boiling water. Cooking spaghetti had always been easy, so why did I have one big clump of pasta in the pot? Obviously, I didn't know what I was doing. This was starting to look like an epic failure.

Utensils. I needed utensils—forks. Watch the spaghetti before it gets to the point of no return.

Not only was I running late, but now I was going to have to serve spaghetti that nobody could eat. This was a lot harder than I had originally thought. I better remember not to volunteer next year. Let somebody else do it.

Finally, it was finished. I looked at the clock. It was 7:30 and the youth group had not arrived yet.

Amazingly, I did have time after all. The stress and driving myself crazy was for nothing. The sauce was done, and the spaghetti had been cooking for thirty-five minutes. It was almost done. I didn't think I had ever cooked spaghetti this long. If they showed up in the next ten minutes, it would look like I timed it perfectly.

The house looked festive. The Christmas tree was beautifully lit, and the table was adorned with a red tablecloth and holiday candles, which added a nice touch.

The phone on the wall rang. It was Jessie, my fifteen-year-old daughter. "Hi, Mom. Are you ready? We're on our way, and there are forty-two of us."

"Yes, dear, I'm ready. Come on over."

At 8:00, the house was filled with laughter and singing. It was wall-to-wall people, and they were hungry. I had never seen so much spaghetti disappear in such a short period of time. Good thing I didn't wait to eat until they left, since they didn't even leave one meatball.

"Mom, it's cold out there, and I've been freezing all night," complained Nikki. "Will you take us in your car to the next house?"

"Nikki, you should have taken a coat. No wonder you're cold. I won't drive you to the next house. Get a coat and go on the hay wagon with the rest of the kids. You'll be fine," I reassured her.

The hay wagon wasn't really a hay wagon. It was a six-teen-foot flatbed trailer being pulled by a pickup truck. The hay bales had been strategically placed to give everybody a place to sit and to give that old-fashioned feeling of a real hayride.

"Mom, please. It's too cold, and your car will be warm."

"Nikki, I'm not going to the next house." The firmness in my voice told her I was serious. "I have to clean up here, and besides, I need to get up at four in the morning to go to work. Now, go on the hay wagon with the rest of the kids and have fun. I'll probably be asleep when you get home."

My vivacious thirteen-year-old could be uncooperative at times, but she finally agreed to go with the others.

The phone rang. It was my sister, Brenda, calling from Florida.

"What are you doing? Having a party?"

"No, it's the youth from our church. They're having a progressive dinner and caroling tonight. I was the one who got to cook the spaghetti. Hold on a minute, I have to say goodbye. They're leaving."

It was always fun to see how many teenagers I could get to hug me.

I noticed Nikki had grabbed a blanket. Good, she'll stay warm.

Jacquee was my energetic little six-year-old, with big blue eyes and strawberry blonde hair down to her waist. Strawberry freckles danced across her cheeks and nose. Her little arms went around me, and she gave me a big hug and kiss good-bye.

She wasn't supposed to be part of this event, but since her two older sisters were in the youth group, and they were leaving before I got home, the pastor and his wife agreed to let her come along and be their little mascot for the evening. Even though I tried to convince Jacquee to stay with me for this last round, she was really into this caroling-and-eating thing that the big kids got to do. The only thing left to eat was dessert, and she didn't want to miss out on that. They were going to serve hot chocolate too. Oh well, I tried.

"Okay, I'm back. So, what's up? How've you been?" The conversation was your typical long-distance sister call.

A scream interrupted us. I couldn't concentrate on what my sister was saying as I strained to hear what was going on outside.

The door burst open. Four young people screamed, "Call 9-1-1, call 9-1-1. Your daughter's been run over!"

"Which daughter?"

"Just call 9-1-1."

My sister, sensing the seriousness, said good-bye, and hung up.

With a calm I cannot explain, I called 9-1-1.

Jessie and the pastor's wife ran through the doorway. In a panic, Jessie yelled to call 9-1-1.

"Jessie, who got run over?"

"Nikki and Jacquee." Her eyes were filled with fear.

"Both of them?" It felt unreal that this could really be happening, yet I wasn't afraid.

"9-1-1, what's your emergency?" The voice came over the phone.

"My two children have been run over in front of my house." I sounded too calm—almost silly, as if I was making a joke.

"What's the address and phone number you're calling from?"

I answered her questions.

"Are the children breathing and conscious?"

"I don't know." I looked at the pastor's wife. "Are they breathing and conscious?"

"Yes."

I told the operator, and she asked me another question which I couldn't answer. I handed the phone to the pastor's wife and started to run out the door when somebody grabbed me by the arm. I thought for a split second they were going to prevent me from going to my girls. Instead, the person handed me a coat.

I ran down my long driveway praying, "Lord, You wouldn't allow this to happen to my children unless You were planning to use it in a mighty way. I trust You."

In my weakness, I had strength. The Lord was with me. I felt His presence and His peace that surpasses all understanding.

Pastor Rob had Nikki's head in his lap, and Jacquee was lying next to her trying to get up. Pastor Rob gently explained to Jacquee why she should stay lying down and not move.

I was there in an instant. "Jacquee, Mommy is here, baby." I leaned over and spoke softly. "Please don't get up. You need to stay very still, okay?"

I looked over my shoulder at my older daughter. "Nikki, what happened?"

"The blanket got caught in the wheel and pulled us off."

"Are you hurt?"

"Yea, my leg was under the tire, and I was yelling, 'Get it off. It's on my leg. Get it off!'"

"Okay, Nikki," I soothed. "You probably broke your leg. It's okay. We're going to get you to the hospital."

"Mommy, it hurts. It really hurts bad, and I can't feel my feet."

"I know, sweetheart. I know. It's going to hurt. You got run over."

Jacquee cried softly, "Mommy, my arms hurt."

"Well, you might have broken them."

"My face hurts and my chest, too," Jacquee whimpered. "Everything hurts, Mommy!"

"Okay, the ambulance is coming. We called 9-1-1."

"What's taking them so long? Tell them to hurry up. It hurts, Mommy. It hurts."

"They're coming sweetie. Can you hear them? They're coming."

The sirens and the red flashing lights arrived. I looked up and saw people lining the street.

Pastor Mark came near us and asked, "Are you okay?"

I looked at him with that peace that surpasses all understanding, and said, "I'm fine, just fine."

He searched my eyes and must have known it was true.

The paramedics worked on my girls, asking them all kinds of questions. They took scissors and cut their clothes. They put a neck brace on Jacquee. They talked about airlifting them.

Inside my home, there was hugging, crying, and praying by those who were unfortunate witnesses of this frightening accident. Outside, the rain that had been forecast that evening held back, and a gentle snow began to fall. It seemed as if a dusting of heavenly blessing fell on us.

The prayer chains started. God's strength and peace continued to stay with me.

My husband wasn't home. Jessie tried his beeper but got no answer. He was out Christmas shopping, and it might be a while before he came home. But maybe, just maybe, he stopped by one of his buddies' houses. Jessie started calling around to see if she could locate him.

Seeing how the winds were now blowing about thirty miles an hour, the paramedics decided that the girls could make the thirty-minute ambulance ride to the hospital. I was glad they weren't putting my babies in a helicopter.

The paramedics loaded Jacquee and Nikki into the ambulance, and I climbed in the front next to the driver. The snow stopped, and it started to rain. The windshield was a kaleidoscope of reflections.

Thank You, Lord, for holding off the rain and keeping my babies dry.

The driver looked over at me, "Are you okay?" He started up his vehicle and pulled away slowly. The wipers flapped out a rhythm, and the windshield kaleidoscope disappeared with each swipe of the blades.

"Yea, I'm fine." My mind swirled with so many thoughts. Why am I not crying? I must be in shock. I'll probably cry tomorrow. How had they both fallen off the hay wagon? Where had they been sitting? Did Jessie see the whole thing? I wondered if Jessie was okay?

"God, they are alive," I silently prayed. "Be with them. Help them not to feel too much pain. Give them courage. Give me courage, Lord. Help me through this. And where is Jack? Why isn't he home?"

The driver looked over at me again. "Are you sure you're okay?"

"Yea, I'm just praying."

The streets were wet and the pavement uneven. I worried that the girls were hurting with every jostle of the ambulance. I looked over my shoulder to see how they were doing.

The paramedics were busy doing their job. There were IVs running into my babies' little veins. They seemed to be doing well considering all they had been through. Jacquee was still faintly crying. She sounded like she had no energy left.

"I want to go to sleep," I heard her weak voice say.

"No, honey, you have to stay awake," the paramedic said softly.

"Why can't I go to sleep? I want to go to sleep." She struggled to keep her eyes open.

"Jacquee, do you remember when Alex fell off the swing set, and they told her not to go to sleep?" Nikki was trying to keep her sister awake. "Remember, they said if she went to sleep, she might not wake up for a long time?"

"Yea."

"Well, that's why they don't want you to go to sleep. Okay, Jacquee? Stay awake. Try hard to stay awake."

"Okay, Nikki. I will."

I wished I could be back there with them, but I was glad they had each other.

The long, dark desert road was lit by streetlights. We were coming into the outskirts of town. It would be only a few more minutes, and we would arrive at the hospital. The driver maneuvered his vehicle with the skill of a well-trained expert. I found myself amazed at the grace and ease in which he avoided others on the road who failed to see the ambulance or hear the sirens.

We pulled into the driveway of the hospital and wove our way around to the emergency entrance. Doctors and nurses were waiting for our arrival as we pulled up.

They took Jacquee in first because of the extent of her injuries.

"Jacquee, remember, be brave," was Nikki's advice as they pulled Jacquee's gurney off the ambulance. "I'm right behind you."

"Okay, Nikki, I'll be brave. I love you."

"I love you, too, Jacquee."

The doctors and nurses started their procedures, and the admitting nurse got all the pertinent information from me. I signed the forms, then asked if I could use the emergency room phone.

The phone barely rang, and Jessie answered with anticipation in her voice.

"Jessie, have you found Daddy yet?"

"No, Mommy. I have tried everybody."

"Well, I'll keep calling throughout the night, so you'll know what's happening. How are you doing?"

"I'm okay. How are Jacquee and Nikki?"

"They look like they are going to be okay, but I don't know yet. Like I said, I'll call you as soon as I know something. I've got to go, sweetie. Good-bye."

The hospital was clean and smelled of antiseptic. I looked at Jacquee under the bright lights of the emergency room, and for the first time I noticed that there was a definite tire mark across the left side of her face. It continued over her neck and right shoulder. That's when I realized there were probably internal injuries. I needed to brace myself for the worst.

With her little face racked with pain, Jacquee looked up at me and said, "Mommy, my heart hurts, and it hurts to breathe."

This could be serious. She could die. I bowed my head and silently prayed, "Oh, Lord, I consecrated this child to You once, and I consecrate her to You again. I realize that all our days are numbered and sometimes six-year-olds die. If this is the day that Jacquee is to go home to heaven and be with You, then You will have to give me strength to get through it. You love her more than I do, but I want to keep her, Lord."

At that moment the Lord spoke to my spirit. "Lay hands on the sick and they shall be healed."

I reached over and put my hand on Jacquee's chest and prayed, "Lord, You told us to lay hands on the sick, and they shall be healed. I claim this Scripture over Jacquee right now. And I believe Your Word is true, for You cannot lie. If You lie, then You are not God. Father, if there is anything wrong in this little body, I pray You heal her. In Jesus's name. Amen."

It was time to take the girls to get x-rayed. They advised me that Jacquee would be awhile because they were going to take her for CAT scans and x-rays. They injected medicine into her IV tube, which would help her relax. I watched as they wheeled my daughters away.

Some of our acquaintances were out in the waiting room of the ER. I looked across the hall and through the small window that revealed the waiting room area. There were several concerned faces looking back. I went over to them, and they rushed to my side for any news I could share.

I was surprised to see Nikki's teacher, Mrs. Sills, there. I wondered how she found out so fast.

Pastor Mark and Pastor Rob were there, for which I was grateful. My dear friend, Clarabelle, was also there with a supportive hug. She was the person I dumped on whenever things got rough. Several other ladies from church were there to offer their support. How reassuring and comforting it was to have my church family with me.

I told them that the girls had gone to x-ray, and we wouldn't know anything until they got back. I shared Jacquee's condition with them and my concern. It was a given that Nikki's leg was broken.

"We are all praying," someone said. "There are ten prayer chains interceding for your girls and three churches that are aware of what is going on. They're all praying."

"Thank you so much. I don't know what I would do if I didn't have all your love and support. Please tell everybody thank you so much." I was touched by all the compassion being poured out on my family.

Nikki returned from x-ray about a half hour later. I told her Mrs. Sills was in the waiting room.

"Can she come in here?" Nikki asked.

"I don't know. Let me find out."

I went out into the hall to see if I could find somebody to ask. I found a nurse nearby. "May we have another person in our room?"

"You are allowed one adult for each child," she said with a smile.

I returned to Nikki's room and told her what the nurse had said. "Do you want Mrs. Sills in here?"

"Yes, please go get her for me." She obviously felt pretty special.

I made my way to the double doors into the waiting room. "Nikki wants you in here with her, Mrs. Sills. It sure would help me. Do you mind?"

Mrs. Sills looked as though she felt honored and nodded her head as if to say, of course.

We made our way back to Nikki whose eyes lit up when she saw her teacher. Mrs. Sills's face beamed as she walked over to Nikki and saw that she was okay. The teacher greeted her with a big hug and kiss.

I marveled at the bonding that had taken place since the first of the school year. I remembered all the trouble Nikki had in the big public school and how so many times the teachers seemed not to like her. I silently thanked the Lord for all He had accomplished in this small Christian school of less than two hundred students.

A doctor entered the room and asked if I was the mother.

"Yes," I said, hoping we'd finally get some answers.

"Well, this young lady's leg is not broken. It's just badly bruised and scraped up. We'll clean her up, and she can go home."

We were all surprised and happy at the news. Nikki praised the Lord in her own humorous way. "See, God does make durable materials. I didn't break."

Mrs. Sills and I laughed with her. We talked about how there was an angel somewhere wearing Nikki's war wounds and how thankful we were that God had protected her.

As we laughed and made small talk, I thought about Jacquee. Is she going to be okay? If there was an angel on the scene, then it must have protected both girls. But those tire marks across her swollen face were all I could see in my mind.

"Where is Jacquee?" I asked almost an hour later when a nurse came into Nikki's room. "Why is it taking so long?"

"CAT scans take a long time. They are almost through. She'll be back soon." The nurse was kind and patient.

We talked about what had happened and how it happened. I kept looking to see if Jacquee was back.

Two hours later, a nurse finally poked her head around the door and told me Jacquee was in her room and asking for me.

I kissed Nikki and rushed to Jacquee's side. After a peck on the cheek, I said, "How are you feeling?" I thought she looked awful.

"I'm okay. I had to go in a big round thing." She said it as if she had been on an adventure.

"Oh? Were you scared?"

"Nah … it wasn't scary."

An hour later the doctor walked in and examined Jacquee's face, shoulder, and hand.

"Did this happen on a dirt road?" He asked with a puzzled look on his face.

"No, sir. It happened on the black top in front of my home."

"I don't understand. This child's face should be crushed, and she should be fighting for her life, but we can't find a broken bone in her face."

"Praise God." The words burst out of my grateful heart. "Well, doctor, I'd say there was an angel between her face and that tire."

"This is hard to believe. This should be on *Amazing Stories* or something." His gaze returned to Jacquee, and he said, "Somebody saved you tonight, young lady."

Jacquee spoke matter-of-factly, "I know who saved me."

"Really? Who saved you?" the doctor asked.

Jacquee smiled and said, "Jesus saved me."

The doctor explained that the x-rays and CAT scans showed no swelling on the brain. There were two small punctures in the lungs, but they were so small that they didn't show up on the x-rays. They found the punctures when they did the CAT scan. He explained how her little chest collapsed like an accordion and bounced back, yet they couldn't even find a broken rib. Her lungs were bruised, and she would be sore for a while. Three bones in Jacquee's hand were broken, but those were clean breaks and would only take three weeks to heal. No surgery was required.

The doctor wanted to keep her in the hospital for one or two days for observation. I agreed, but I was fairly certain they wanted to admit her because they couldn't believe there was nothing wrong with her. They wanted to be sure nothing had been missed.

The doctor walked away to make the arrangements to admit Jacquee into the hospital and release Nikki to go home.

A few steps took me to Jacquee's bedside. I bent over her to look more closely at my daughter. My heart burst with thankfulness that she was still with us. Smoothing free a whisp of her hair that was stuck to her facial wound, I said, "Hey, little girl, you scared me tonight. I thought you were going home to heaven to be with Jesus."

"Oh, Mommy, I'm glad I didn't because I wouldn't have been able to say good-bye to Daddy and Jessie."

It was 12:30 a.m. at this point. I called Jessie one more time. "Did Daddy ever make it home?"

"Yea, he got home a few minutes ago."

In an earlier conversation, I told her not to let her daddy come to the hospital because we might be on our way home, and I didn't want us missing each other.

"He wants to talk to you. But first, how are Nikki and Jacquee?"

"They are fine. Nikki is coming home, but Jacquee has to stay in the hospital for a day or two for observation. But she's okay. They couldn't find anything wrong with her head or chest. Just her hand is broken."

"Oh, good. I'll get Daddy." She sounded relieved to know her sisters were going to be okay.

"What's up? What happened? How did this happen?" The questions came one after another with no time to answer in between. His voice was a combination of fear and anger. "Are they okay?"

"Everything is fine, dear. It was just an accident, but the kids are fine. They are releasing Nikki right now, and Clarabelle is bringing her home. Jacquee has to stay for a day or two for observation. They will probably let her come home tomorrow because they can't find anything broken except her hand."

"I'm on my way. I'll be there as soon as possible."

"Wait, honey, don't leave yet. Wait until Nikki gets home. See that she gets settled and into bed, and then come."

It was about an hour later when Jack showed up at the hospital. We were still in the ER and waiting for them to put Jacquee in a room. She was sleeping soundly when her daddy bent down with tears in his eyes and kissed her on the forehead. "Jacquee, Jacquee. Daddy is here."

"Hi, Daddy."

"How are you, pumpkin?"

"I got runned over."

"I see that. I'm glad you're okay. Go to sleep. Your daddy is here now." She dozed off again. He looked up at me and asked, "How did this happen?"

I explained the events of the evening. He apologized for not being there. We held each other and were thankful for all our blessings.

Even though Jack was very upset and wanted to blame somebody, I realized that God kept him out of the picture for a reason. The fact that he wasn't there until we knew the girls were okay was nothing less than God's grace. Otherwise, he said he would have punched somebody. Now, we simply leaned on each other and waited to get Jacquee in a room.

Jacquee stayed in the hospital for two days. She had lots of visitors who brought presents and good cheer. Two Santas came by with gifts. DJs from a local radio station visited the children's ward and brought gifts. Two families visiting children in the hospital for Christmas came by and brought gifts for Jacquee. We joked how she was getting two Christmases this year.

The best Christmas present of all was that our Jacquee got to come home Christmas Eve, and our whole family was together. We thanked God for this blessing. We thanked Him for the miracle He had performed on December 22, 1994. We will never forget it.

As I looked back, I realized that in my moment of weakness, I had His strength. God gave me peace that surpassed all understanding, and because I abide in Him, He abides in me.

I thought of Abraham sacrificing Isaac on one of the mountains of Moriah (Genesis 22) and how God tested him. I was tested that night, and my faith held up. Thank You, Lord Jesus. You are truly our Savior, Redeemer, and Rescuer.

Footnote: In case you are wondering as so many do, Jacquee is healthy and happy. She received As and Bs throughout her school years. Her head is not deformed, and she does not suffer from headaches or seizures. There have been no ill effects from this accident. She is a beautiful, thirty-five-year-old wife and mother of three as of 2023.

Chapter 2

For the eyes of the LORD are on the righteous,
And His ears are attentive to their prayer....
(1 PETER 3:12)

Turkey Faith

"Hello," said the voice on the other end of the phone. "Hi, Jennifer, this is Mrs. Powers up the street. Merry Christmas."

"Merry Christmas."

"I'm sorry to be calling so early, but I was wondering if your family could use a turkey. My husband's boss gave it to him last night, and we already have one."

"Can you hold on? I'll go ask my mom."

"Sure, honey." I waited for about three minutes. My thoughts went back to the night before. It was Christmas Eve of 1987.

I was already irritated by the fact that my husband wasn't home from work yet, and it was 11:00 at night. His tradition every year since we got married was to do all his Christmas shopping on Christmas Eve. There was so much to do on Christmas Eve, and morning would come too soon for me.

My beloved arrived around midnight with gifts in tow and a fifteen-pound turkey. I already had a huge turkey in the refrigerator.

"What is this?" I spoke through clenched teeth.

"It's my Christmas bonus."

"Is your boss stupid? Doesn't he realize he needs to tell us in advance if he's going to give us a turkey, so we don't buy one?"

The voice on the other end interrupted my thoughts. "Mrs. Powers, my mom said, yes, she would love to have the turkey."

"Okay, you can come down and pick it up when you're ready."

About a half hour later, there was a knock on the door. I hurried to the kitchen to get the bird out of the refrigerator and opened the front door to hand it to Jennifer, who was standing there with three of her younger siblings.

They were a strange family. They talked about Jesus all the time. The mom never went to work outside the home. The kids had very little. Their shoes had holes, and their clothes were worn out, but they seemed happy.

I was guilty of talking about them and making fun of their Christianity. Deep down, I admired them, but they were different.

"Mrs. Powers, I need to tell you something before I take the turkey."

"Okay."

"My mom was praying all week for a turkey for Christmas dinner. We couldn't afford one, but Mom said she was praying and trusting the Lord for a turkey for Christmas."

Tears filled my eyes. I couldn't believe what I was hearing.

"God chose me to answer your mom's prayer?" I asked.

"Yes, ma'am."

"Thank you for letting me know. Merry Christmas."

I shut the door and sat down on the couch. There must be something real about being a Christian. It seemed God hears the prayers of people who follow Him. I wanted that kind of faith.

It wasn't too long after this incident that I became a Christian. Not only did God use me to answer a faithful woman's prayer, but He used that faithful Christian family to speak to me, and it changed my life.

Chapter 3

Behold, to obey is better than sacrifice…
(1 Samuel 15:22 NKJV)

Chickens on the Commuter Van

The mail room was hustling and bustling. Four-wheeled carts held more than one hundred packages being shipped all over the world. Trays of mail were stacked on the table ready to be picked up by the U.S. Postal Service. Employees frequented the service area to ship their personal packages.

It was December. We had all become used to the pressures of the holiday season. It happened every year.

The phone rang, and I answered it just as I had done thirty other times that day. "Mail Services, this is Debbie."

"Do you have somebody who can help out on the loading dock for about forty-five minutes?" the voice on the other end asked.

"I don't know. We are busy down here. Who is this?" I asked with a matter-of-fact attitude. Somebody always wants us to do something—pick up something or take something somewhere. I was used to not giving in on the first request.

"Oh, I'm sorry. This is Diane in Personnel," the manager said.

"What do you have on the loading dock?" I asked with a little more respect.

"Chickens. Two thousand pounds of chickens." She spoke in all seriousness.

"What? Chickens? Why do you have two thousand pounds of chickens on the loading dock?" I laughed. "And what are you going to do with them?" Since I worked for Sunkist, oranges on the loading dock would have been understandable, but chickens?

"It seems one of the trucking companies we use was going up the freeway and was pulled into the weigh station," the manager said. "They informed the woman driving the truck that she had to unload two thousand pounds before she would be permitted to continue. She called the transportation manager and asked if she could give us two thousand pounds of chickens. Apparently, she didn't have time to go back to her original loading spot, and we would be doing her a favor," Diane said.

"So, what are we going to do with them?" I asked.

"We're going to give every employee a chicken. It'll be a nice and unexpected Christmas bonus."

"Okay, I'll see who I can get out there to help."

For the next two hours, several employees unload naked chickens and wrapped them in plastic bags. The announcement went out over the intercom to pick up your free chicken in the cafeteria. When the mad dash for free chickens was over, there were still chickens left.

This is where God and I had our conversation.

God: Ask for the chickens for the food ministry.

Me: I don't want to ask for the chickens, God. I'm always asking for stuff for our church.

God: Ask for the chickens.

Me: But God, I'm in a vanpool, remember?

God: Ask for the chickens.

Me: It will be a hassle getting them home. (I lived sixty miles away.)

God: Ask for the chickens.

Me: Okay, okay. I'll ask for the chickens. But I hope they don't give them to me. I have enough on my plate without worrying about getting chickens to the food ministry.

I picked up the phone and called. Before giving us the chickens, Diane wanted me to make sure that my church wanted the chickens and had a place to put them.

I called Debbie Hall, the leader of the food ministry. "So, Debbie, the story is that there was this truck going up the freeway when it got pulled into the weigh station and had to get rid of two thousand pounds. The trucker called Sunkist and asked if she could unload two thousand pounds of chickens at our facility. Every employee has received a free chicken," I rambled on.

Debbie was laughing. "Why are you telling me this?"

"Well, you see, there are somewhere between fifty and eighty chickens left over, and God made me ask for them for the food ministry. Sunkist wants to make sure you want them and have a place to put them before they donate them to the food ministry."

Debbie became excited. I could imagine her jumping up and down while she called her husband, Sam, into the room.

She said, "Sam and I had just been talking about how wonderful it would be to have chickens to put in the food baskets. We prayed specifically for chickens. We were hoping we could think of a way to get some."

"I guess I was supposed to ask for the chickens because God was answering your prayer." I hung my head in shame.

"Praise God!" Debbie said excitedly. "He is so good."

"All the time," I said.

But that's not the end of my story. No, indeed. I had to find a way to get all those chickens home. Lucky for me, four of the eight people who rode in our vanpool weren't on the van that day. We put chickens on the seats, under the seats, and in the back of the seats.

The chickens were partially frozen, and we didn't want them to thaw, so we decided it would be wise to keep the heater off. We talked to the frozen chickens on our long drive: "Please don't thaw. Stay cool, little fellas."

Then a thought occurred to me. What if we got pulled over? How would we explain these chickens? Would the police think we were smuggling drugs inside the chickens? We could see the headlines now, "Chickens on the Commuter Van." The story would tell how the police searched every chicken and found no "fowl" play.

What I feared would turn into a big hassle, turned out not to be much of a hassle after all. We had a few laughs, and the memory of that day will be with us for a long time. It turned out that there were fifty-nine chickens in all. That week God blessed families with plump fresh chickens for their holiday meals.

Chapter 4

Many are the plans in a person's heart,
but it is the LORD's purpose that prevails.
(PROVERBS 19:21)

The Job I Didn't Want

I was unemployed for a year, so when the employment agency I applied with called me about a job interview, I jumped at the opportunity. There had been several that I thought would be perfect for me. However, I didn't get them. This one was a little farther than I wanted to drive, but a job is a job, and I would take whatever I could get.

I drove the deserted road across the desert behind Edwards Air Force Base. After driving about thirty minutes, I told myself it's not that bad. I remembered the days of commuting in traffic sixty miles one way. There definitely was no traffic on this road.

Then I crested the hill and viewed the massive Mojave floor. For as far as the eyes could see, there was desert, and off in the distance was the Borax Mine. This was my destination for the job prospect. It looked unwelcoming, isolated, and remote.

Surely, Lord, this is not where You want me to work. It's so ugly. But Your will, not mine.

I reached my destination and entered the plant. It was even uglier up close. I didn't want to work in a place that was so unappealing. But I reminded myself, God's will, not my will be done.

Dressed to impress, I checked in at the guard shack. I watched a safety video. Another lady was there for the same position. We were both escorted to the Administration Building by a gentleman who would be interviewing us. He advised us to stay inside the marked crosswalks and hold the handrails when going up or down stairs. He informed us that we might hear a blast, but not to be startled because it was heard around there all the time. He explained it was the miners dynamiting the borates out of the open pit mine.

He took the other lady in first for her interview, and I waited in the lobby. Soon it was my turn. As I ascended the stairs, I held the handrail wondering how many germs I was touching. However, there were sanitizer dispensers on the wall at the top and bottom of the stairs.

I decided I wouldn't try too hard to impress in the interview. Although I'd never had such an attitude during any interview in the past, this time that's what I did. If God wanted me to have this job, He would have to accomplish it without my help.

The position consisted of working two part-time jobs. Four hours in the morning in Customer Service and four hours in the afternoon in Occupational Health. Both department managers were interviewing at the same time.

I answered each question as negatively as I could, hoping I would fail miserably and not be chosen. As I drove home, I was sure I had succeeded in doing just that.

I was only in the door a few minutes when the phone rang, and the employment agency told me they wanted to offer the job to me. Go figure.

But God's will had been done, and I was about to embark on a journey of blessings.

Within a year I was given a one dollar raise. Within the next year, I was promoted and given three dollars more an hour.

At that point, my prayer was that they would hire me as an employee, because I was still a temp. Well, that opportunity emerged.

I asked God that if I got the job, could I at least be offered what I was making when I left my old job as an assistant manager at Sunkist, which would be an additional five dollars per hour. I knew I was asking a lot, but you have not because you ask not, right? I was three years in by this point, and I had already been blessed financially beyond anything I could have imagined. Unfortunately, if they didn't hire me, I would be unemployed since they had too many temporary workers, and they were told that the company needed to either hire them or let them go.

God was good. I was hired and offered six dollars more an hour. A dollar more than I had prayed for.

The blessings didn't stop there. They had a program for new hires. Vacation time was allotted to new employees based on the number of years of experience you had and not the number of years working for the company. Based on my years of experience in administrative work, I was given five weeks of vacation a year.

I worked for twenty-three years at Sunkist and only earned four weeks of vacation annually. Five weeks of vacation was unheard of as far as I was concerned. I was blown away by another blessing from the hand of God.

How glad I was that God's will had been accomplished, and He overrode my initial prayer. I ended up loving my job.

Chapter 5

*Count it all joy, my brothers, when you meet trials of various
kinds, for you know that the testing of your faith produces
steadfastness. And let steadfastness have its full effect, that
you may be perfect and complete, lacking in nothing.*
(JAMES 1: 2–4 ESV)

Answered Prayer

One of the most difficult times in my life was when my
husband was unemployed for six months. He worked
in construction, so we had faced dry patches in the past.
That's just the way the industry works. But never six months.
A week or two or even a month we could squeak by, but six
months was brutal.

We had no savings. We had lots of debt, and it was hard
to make ends meet. We stopped paying unnecessary bills like
credit cards and loans.

Although I was working, I only made half of what my
husband made. The stress was awful. I prayed and prayed and
prayed, until I was all prayed up.

I was angry at God for not supplying a job for my husband. God had promised to supply our needs. So why were
we going through this?

My girlfriends at church were praying, and it was comforting to know they were helping me carry this burden. One day I cried to one of these precious ladies, and she told me, "Don't stop praying."

I became upset with her and told her, "I'm tired of praying. I don't want to pray anymore."

She wasn't offended but continued to love me and told me it was okay. She assured me of her continued prayers for my situation.

Finally, the prayers were answered, and after six months, my husband found work. Hallelujah! Thank You, Jesus.

However, the most interesting part of this story is what led up to this difficult time.

Debt can ruin years of our lives. I was troubled about the debt we had accumulated. I had attended several events where the subject was discussed, and we were taught about how to rid ourselves of debt. I learned that debt robs us of God's blessings. This made sense. It felt right to work toward the goal of becoming debt-free.

However, I couldn't do it without my husband. I told him it was essential for us to work on reducing our debt. He said that debt was the American way. Everybody is in debt. We will die in debt.

With that answer, it seemed it would be an uphill battle. My husband was not easily influenced by me. The only thing I could do was pray.

My prayer was, Lord, help my husband to see that we need to be out of debt.

Little did I know how God was going to answer my prayer. After being unemployed for six months, my husband changed his attitude and understood our finances from a different perspective.

It took months, maybe years, to get a handle on our spending and pay down all the credit cards. It seemed like a mountain we couldn't climb, but we climbed it one step at a time. We were more focused and deliberate about our spending. Did we always make good financial decisions? I wish I could say yes, but we did better than we had in the past.

Once we got our debt under control, the stress was also under control.

God had directed this entire process. It had been difficult to go through, but it was necessary. Bottom line, God answered both prayers. He didn't make it easy, but He knew what it would take for my husband and me to agree about our finances.

Chapter 6

When my father and my mother forsake me,
Then the LORD will take care of me.
(PSALM 27:10 NKJV)

The Lord Loved Me the Moment I Was Conceived

This is not a story I want to tell. I share it in hope that through my story you can overcome too.

The Lord loved me the moment I was conceived, even before, as He does all of us. My journey began with two imperfect people in an imperfect world but a perfect God.

Who knows what a baby goes through while in the mother's womb? My mother liked to drink and smoke. Some mothers do drugs. It must have some kind of effect on the unborn child, thus the beginning of an imperfect life.

Some children are fortunate enough to have parents who care more about them than they care about themselves. These children can't fully appreciate what they have.

I wasn't one of those fortunate children. My parents were selfish. This made for scary and insecure early years. How children like me learn to survive is a God-given gift. When I think of how God was always with me, I am grateful.

Rick was my brother. I have few memories of him as a child, but the ones I do have are pleasant. Rick was my buddy, my play pal. He was older, and I remember we played together. I don't recall ever fighting with him over toys or anything else. I think he was a good big brother.

As far as childhood memories, how much of what we remember is correct? How much is inaccurate? Why do we remember the things we remember, and why do we forget the things we forget?

As children, we often sat on the hardwood floor in the dining room, with Rick playing in front of the china cabinet. We played, colored, and behaved like children without a care in the world. At least that's how I remember it. However, Rick remembered things differently. He said, while we played in the dining room, Mom and Dad would be fighting in the kitchen. Dad often hit Mom. I don't remember that, but how frightening it would be to remember it.

My memories are about the abuse I received at my mother's hand. There was the time when I was two or three years old, and Mom picked me up by my arm and threw me across the room onto a couch to get me out of her way. She was angry, and it scared me. I started crying. My dad apparently saw it and went after her. I heard him slapping her in the other room. I remember being glad that she was getting a spanking for doing that to me.

Speaking of spankings, another incident that sticks out in my memory is when I got the belt. I was still very young, maybe three or four years old. I said the "N" word. But where did I learn that horrible word? Mom whipped me until I peed my pants. The unfortunate thing was, I was lying across her bed receiving my punishment. I didn't tell her I peed, and when she discovered the wetness on her bed, I got another spanking.

Now as an adult, I sometimes try to remember something good about those early years. Not much comes to mind. Only that my mom looked pretty when my dad and she went out and that Dad looked handsome.

As far as Christmas memories, I had none. Birthday memories? None. Security? No. Loved? No. Scared? I think so.

Much of what happens in our childhood molds us and shapes us into the people we will become. The good thing about God's gift of a free will is that we can choose to be bitter people, or we can choose to be better people because of what we have experienced.

The day my mother left, I was four years old. She lied to me. She packed the car and told us we were going to visit Grandma. Instead, she took my brother, Rick, and left, never to return.

She told me she was going to the store, and she would be right back. She said she would bring me bubble gum. I must have waited hours at the big picture window in our living room watching as each car went by, but none of them were my mom's car. I fell asleep at that window. The babysitter must have picked me up and put me in my bed. When I awoke the next morning, I was told that Mommy had run away.

The day my daddy left, I was probably five years old. I don't remember what happened between my mom leaving and my dad leaving. However, I do remember standing at the front door of our house. Daddy stooped down on one knee and tried to explain why he was going away. I was scared and cried. He hugged me, and then he was gone.

For the next four years, until I was nine years old, I lived with my Aunt Allie and Uncle Pete. My other brother, Theo, and my little sister, Brenda, also lived there. Chores, school, and homework were most of what I remember. A few of the good memories of that period in my life were playing with my cousins, playing with my dolls, playing in the backyard, roller skating at Swan Lake, and running around the lake. Even then, I don't remember birthday or Christmas celebrations. We must have had them because there were seven kids in total. I can only assume they weren't very impressive since I can't recall any of them.

The day came at nine years old that my little brother, little sister, grandfather (Popoo), and I got on a plane and left my aunt and uncle's home in South Carolina. Our five-hour journey took us to Los Angeles where we were finally reunited with Daddy. We arrived in "Sunny Southern California" to a small bachelor apartment. I was the happiest I had ever been. I had my daddy back. He was my knight in shining armor.

I stepped into the role of "lady of the house." I dusted, did the dishes, and took care of my little brother and sister. Dad and Popoo helped, but I was the oldest and a female. I had responsibilities; at least, that is the way I saw it.

Within days we moved to a larger bungalow in the same apartment complex. I was home. I was happy. There were other kids, and we played outside for hours. Dad went off to work every day, and Popoo was the adult left to watch over us. We must have looked odd to the outside world—no woman in the home and two men raising three small children, ages three, five, and nine. Life was good. Little did I know how this situation would affect my whole life.

Much later, I found out how we ended up in California with our dad. Apparently, my mother had called my aunt and said she would be arriving to pick up her children. After that phone conversation, my aunt spoke to her brother, my dad. Arrangements were made to put us on a plane and send us to California so my mother would not get us. I guess you could say my dad stole us and hid us from my mom. My aunt was his accomplice, and they pulled it off.

When my mom showed up to get us, we were gone. My aunt would not tell her where we were. It is my understanding that Mom looked for us through a private investigator for five years but could never find us.

I wouldn't have wanted to be with my mom. She frightened me. I was so happy to be with my dad.

The day came when I lost my innocence. I was violated. A new and frightening world opened to me. One minute I was playing outside—running and laughing—and the next minute I was in an unknown world.

The one thing I did know and learned early on in life was not to question adults. You obey, and you never talk back. As a child, you have no opinions or rights. What the adults say is what you do. There are no options. I didn't know any better. Like everything else in life, you may not like it, but you do it anyway. Like your chores or brushing your teeth or doing homework. We don't get to do what we want. We do what we must. There are rules, and kids don't make the rules—adults do. And you don't question them.

It started with a newspaper article. My popoo called me in from outside to read me this newspaper article. It was about a girl who got raped.

Raped? What was that? I had never heard that word before. The article didn't make sense to me. So, I asked, "What is raped?" I don't remember Popoo's exact words, but I do remember his actions. I remember him showing and touching. I remember my life changed that day. Suddenly I knew things, saw things, and felt things I never had. I was nine, and he was my grandfather. Why did he think it was okay to introduce me to this world?

Of course, I now know he wasn't teaching me anything. He was indulging his selfish pleasures. He was old and did not have a way to meet women. I was the closest thing to what he needed. I became his victim.

He told me I could not tell anybody, or he would be in trouble. So, I didn't tell. This continued for years. The sad thing is I never told, not until I was an adult. The other sad thing is, he would pay me. I liked having money. All I had to do was endure a few minutes of touchy-feely until he was satisfied, and I received two dollars.

It disgusts me now. Writing this makes me sick. It makes me sad for that little girl. But she survived.

At twelve years old, the sexual molestation stopped because my grandfather suffered a stroke. He lived as a vegetable for the rest of his life. His miserable existence went on for several years. It appeared God didn't allow him to die, at least not for a long time. If there is a purgatory, I think that is it.

Like father, like son. The nightmare was back. Drunk and self-consumed, my father became my new predator. My daddy, my knight in shining armor—how could this be?

He didn't have to show me how to do it. I had already been through the training. I don't remember when it started. Was I twelve? Was it after Popoo got sick and went away? Or did it start before my grandfather got sick? It's all a blur.

It was always late at night, him standing over my bed and waking me. He wouldn't go away until the deed was done. It was so ugly. It wasn't like Popoo's. It scared me. It never stopped until I was fifteen years old. It only stopped because one night it went too far. It went way too far.

Alcohol is an evil force, and Daddy was drunk. He drove home drunk most nights. He was a bartender. I'm not certain how his evenings progressed, but I imagine he either started drinking before his shift was over, or he went out partying after he got off at 2:00 a.m.

Justifying his actions must have been easier while intoxicated.

To this day, I can't stand drunks. The smell, the behavior, the whole scene—I hate it.

I had a problem with men, too. What was going on in my soul? What was going on in my spirit?

The choices we make as adults affect the children in our lives more than we realize. We need to be ever so mindful of our responsibilities to them. Even then, in our best efforts, we sometimes fail. Despite our best intensions, it can turn out all wrong. However, when we make an obvious bad choice, it can never turn out good. There will be hurt and pain. There will be wounded souls and spirits.

For each victim, the day will arrive when they must make the difficult choice of whether to become bitter or better. Most will choose bitter. Some will encounter God and become better and use their experience to help others. With God's help, we become better and forgive the wrongs done to us. Without God it is impossible. With God all things are possible.

As far as my dad, I often wondered if he felt any shame or guilt. Did he grieve over his actions? Did he feel regret? I wondered if he ever wanted to talk about it, or did he prefer to bury it and hope it all went away. Maybe he was proud of what he'd done and never found fault with himself. I wondered…

After writing the manuscript for this book, I gave it to my dad to read. He was in his late eighties at that point.

He didn't deny anything. Instead, he apologized for what his father had done. He also apologized for what he did to me.

Before allowing him to read this manuscript, I understood that he might not apologize, but that wasn't why I gave it to him. I wanted him to know that I remembered. The apology was a bonus. He remembered, and he wasn't in denial.

My story is a sad story of a little girl who had many obstacles to overcome. But God was faithful and took all the hurt, abuse, and pain, and He caused good to come out of it. The journey wasn't easy. It was hard work. However, the lessons I learned in my healing process and the depth of relationship with God that I gained by trusting Him, made it all worth it.

I want to tell everyone who's faced a traumatic childhood, that there is healing and hope. I'm living proof of that. Over the years, I've had the privilege of walking other women through their healing process. The devil wants to cause us to feel isolated. But it's of utmost importance to remember, you are not alone. God is ready and willing to heal the broken places in your heart as He did for me and for many others.

Start by finding a support group for healing of childhood trauma. I recommend a Christian one if possible. Also, get involved in a Bible study. With God's help, you can finally be freed from your past and completely healed. The Lord says, "For I know the plans I have for you ... plans to prosper you and not to harm you, plans to give you hope and a future" (Jer. 29:11).

Perhaps you're wondering why God allowed this abuse to happen. I don't have all the answers, but I do know that God has given us all a free will, and some people choose to selfishly do bad things that harm others. Let's not forget who's behind all this evil. The devil, of course. He uses whatever he can to destroy God's creation.

You didn't have a choice about what happened to you, but you can use your God-given free will to choose how you will react. If you stay stuck in your pain, you will become a bitter person. I know because I was that bitter and angry woman. For years I was miserable and made my family miserable too.

The hard work toward healing was painful because I had to face my trauma and push beyond it. But once I started to process my pain and talk about it, the devil lost his power over me. The enemy no longer had a foothold in my life.

One of the hardest things I had to do was to forgive. Yet no matter how hard it was, without forgiveness I couldn't heal.

I saw a saying recently that said, "Forgiving is not forgetting. It's remembering without anger." The only way to remember without anger is when you've truly forgiven. That's not something that will happen overnight. It took me years to be able to truly forgive. No one can do this without the help of the Holy Spirit and a wonderful Christian counselor.

I encourage anyone who has faced something similar, to do the hard work of forgiving, receiving counsel, and journaling about the trauma and pain they endured, so the abuse can no longer have a hold on them. Then they can finally be set free of their past.

Chapter 7

The Class Ring

Mom life. If you are a mom, you know exactly what that phrase entails. I loved my "mom life." Caring for my family was a busy life. Working full time on top of that made for days where I fell into bed at night exhausted, just to get up the next morning and do it all again.

The days flew by and before I knew it, we had a senior in high school. After what seemed like endless laundry, dishes, housework, carpooling kids to all the different activities, school, and homework, I had a senior.

There was a lot of extra money involved with the senior year—prom, yearbook, and class ring. The ring was debatable. Was it necessary? Did she really need it? Would she even wear it?

When all was said and done, we decided she could have one. I believe it was somewhere in the price range of $285.

That was a lot of money out of our household budget, but we made it happen. Jessie was so grateful for her class ring. She did wear it, and I never regretted buying it for her.

One day Jessie came to me with a sad expression on her face. She said she couldn't find her class ring.

I reassured her that it would show up, then I went about my mom duties and didn't think about the ring until three days later when Jessie approached me again. This time she was pretty upset that she still hadn't found the ring.

I drilled her on where she looked. Did you check under your bed? Did you look in your bed. It could have fallen off your finger while you were sleeping. Did you look on your desk? Did you look in your desk? How about your car? Under the seat?

She answered yes to each suggestion. She said she looked everywhere for three days without success.

Jessie asked if I could pray for her to find her ring. "God always hears your prayers, Mom."

I put my arms around her, and she laid her head on my shoulder. I prayed the simplest prayer. "Father, I ask that You help Jessie find her class ring. In Jesus's name. Amen." And with that I went back to what I was doing in the kitchen, and Jessie went down the hall to her room.

The next thing I heard was a bloodcurdling scream. I was sure there was an ax murderer in the house. My heart dropped to the bottom of my stomach, and I took off running toward

Jessie's room. As I exited the kitchen and rounded the corner, I saw her running down the hall holding her ring in her hand.

I raised my gaze to heaven and said, "Gee, that was fast, Lord."

I asked Jessie where she'd found it.

Jessie said, "I walked into my room, and it was sitting in the middle of the floor." She shook her head in disbelief. "Mom, it wasn't there before."

It was as if an angel had taken it out of its hiding place and put it in the middle of Jessie's floor so she would see it.

Chapter 8

You do not have because you do not ask God.
(JAMES 4:2)

Rain, Rain, Go Away

The one thing about working at the mine was, you had to walk quite a distance from the parking lot to the office. About two blocks. On cold days, we bundled up in warm gear.

Mornings in the Mojave Desert could be down in the single digits. On hot days, it could get to 125 degrees by the end of the workday. On rainy days, it was a good idea to bring an umbrella because if there was enough rain to trigger a flash flood warning, you'd look like a drowned rat by the time you made it to your car.

On this day, the forecast was for rain and a lot of it. So being the wise woman that I am, I grabbed my umbrella and headed to work. By the time I arrived, it hadn't started raining yet. As wise as I thought I was, I forgot my umbrella in the car. I didn't think anything of it until it started raining halfway through the day. That's when I remembered my umbrella was in the car. I hoped the rain would slow down before it was time to go home. Otherwise, I would be drenched before I reached my car.

While I packed to leave work, the rain continued pouring. I said a quick prayer. "Lord, please make it stop raining long enough for me to get to my car."

As I headed out, the rain stopped just long enough for me to climb into my car, and then it started coming down again. But I was completely dry.

Chapter 9

Surely, Lord, you who bless the righteous;
you surround them with your favor as with a shield.
(PSALM 5:12)

Game Shows

When I was young and there was no school because of a holiday or I was sick, I would watch *Let's Make a Deal* and *The Price Is Right*. These were my favorite game shows, and I vowed that when I was eighteen years old, I would be on both of these game shows.

When I turned eighteen, I went down to the studio where *Let's Make a Deal* was filmed in hopes of getting selected for the trading floor. I wore a belly dance outfit since *Let's Make a Deal* was a gameshow where you would dress up in a crazy costume, and Monty Hall would select people from the audience to make deals with him. You could win big prizes and sometimes money. People from all over the country would come in costumes, carrying signs that had clever sayings on them in the hopes of receiving attention and being chosen to play. My sign said, "I will shake it all for Monty Hall." Get it? I was dressed like a belly dancer.

I was chosen to be on the trading floor, but that didn't mean Monty Hall would choose me to make a deal.

As it turned out, he did choose me. I was excited. He also chose a couple of men to play the game. All they had to do was guess my weight.

This is so politically incorrect nowadays, but back then it was perfectly acceptable.

The guy that came closest to the correct weight won something, and the other guy had to sit down. Once Monty was done with them, he turned to me and handed me two hundred dollars for being a good sport about it all. Then he offered me the box on the floor if I gave the two hundred dollars back to him. I took the box and ended up with a console stereo and fun furniture, which was basically plastic furniture for outside. I didn't win big, but I won, and I was on national TV.

When I turned nineteen, I was back down at the studios standing in line to get on *The Price Is Right*. The directors interviewed everybody in line. The interview was not a long one. It lasted less than a minute. Truth be told, you were lucky if you got thirty seconds. So, I had to impress right off the bat.

To make the game show fun for the viewing TV audience, the studio looked for people who were not shy and were willing to act a little crazy. I understood that. I was wild and crazy and a little embarrassing, but it worked. My name was called to "Come on down!"

It was exciting and fun, except I got stuck on Contestant's Row, which meant I never bid the right price on any item for the entire show. It was a letdown, but I was on national TV again. And in my defense, I was nineteen years old. What does a nineteen-year-old know about the price of anything.

Fast forward forty years. My dear friend, Rosita, invited me to go with her to *The Price Is Right*. Now I was fifty-nine years old and still loved the show, but I seldom watched it because I worked full time, Monday through Friday. At first, I told Rosita no about attending, but she eventually talked me into it, and I scheduled time off from my job.

We met up with another friend and headed down to the studios where they filmed. It was about an hour drive. Even though Rosita had tickets, they did not guarantee entrance if you weren't one of the first three hundred people. You had to arrive early and stand in line. They counted off and closed the gate behind the three hundredth person.

Then the long process began. Each person was signed in by an individual and given a name tag and a number. Studio personnel handed each of us a release form that we had to read and sign. Basically, it said we would not be reim-bursed if we ended up on camera, and there was no guarantee we would be picked to be on the show.

I noticed where the cameras were placed around the area where we were lined up, watching us. I wondered if they were for security purposes or to see the energy of individuals. We were probably already being auditioned without being aware of it. At least that's what ran through my mind after spotting the cameras.

I started people watching. Looking at the sea of people, I realized that somebody standing here was going to win big today, and they didn't know it, and several will hear the words, "Come on down!"

The next step in the process was to sit in front of a computer and smile. I gave the biggest and cheesiest grin I could. Then they placed each of us in front of a green screen and asked us to react to winning a car as they videotaped our reaction.

We were funneled to the final process of the audition, which was to stand in line side by side. The line included about thirty people, and I was about halfway down the line.

A young lady sat on a stool with her back to us and a clipboard on her lap. A young man walked up to each person and asked what they did for a living.

I started to think about what I was going to say. At that time, I was an export logistics clerk. I didn't want to tell him that. I wanted to say something clever instead. Then I remembered that I was technically a miner since I worked at a mine. Of course, I worked in the office, but it was at a mine, so that made me a miner.

"Hi, Debbie, what do you do for a living?"

"I'm a miner."

"So, you are too young to be on the show?"

"Not that kind of minor. I work in a mine."

He talked to me longer than he had with most people who were waiting in line. I took that as a good sign.

"You work down in a mine?"

"Well, no. I'm actually an export logistic clerk at the mine, but that still makes me a miner. And I'm also an alumnus."

"Oh? An alumnus of what?"

"Of *The Price Is Right*. I was here when I was nineteen years old."

"Well, good luck." He moved on.

The young lady sitting on the stool with the clipboard turned around to look at me and then wrote something.

Rosita said, "Did you see that? She wrote you down. They're gonna call you."

"I saw it. If they do, I hope I don't trip and fall." I chuckled. I could trip over my own two feet. It was a real concern.

This entire preliminary process took about four hours. Then we waited another two hours before they guided us into the studio. We weren't allowed to sit just anywhere. They had strategically seated every person in the audience. It made sense because they wanted all the people they were going to call to "Come on down!" to be spaced throughout the studio. They led my two friends and me to the very back row in the center of the room.

It was time to start. The energy was electrifying. Everybody was screaming and waving their hands. The first four contestants were called down, and I was not one of them. The product was brought out and the first four contestants took their turn guessing the price. Once the first round was over, they took a commercial break.

Back from the break, I heard, "Debbie Powers, come on down. You are the next contestant on *The Price Is Right!*" Of course, I was thrilled and took off running, screaming, and waving my arms. The whole time, I was thinking, don't fall. I made it safely to Contestant's Row without incident.

During the first round, I didn't bid correctly. In the second round, I didn't bid correctly. I feared I was going to get stuck on Contestant's Row again.

You would think that a fifty-nine-year-old woman would have a good idea about what things cost. I was obviously still not good at this game forty years later. So, I did what I knew how to do, and when they went to the commercial break, I stood at the podium and prayed. "Lord, please don't let me get stuck on Contestant's Row again. Help me to bid correctly on something." I didn't pray that I would win. I only asked God to help me make a correct bid on something.

God answered my prayer. When we came back from the commercial break, I bid correctly and ran up the five steps to the stage to meet Drew Carey ... and I fell. That's right. I biffed it on national TV.

Drew couldn't stop laughing, and neither could I. But the show had to go on. At this point I didn't care if I won anything else. God had answered my prayer.

The game was rolled out onto the stage, and Drew explained how it worked. I didn't understand and asked for him to explain it again. They literally had to cut out a big chunk because I was clueless. I finally just said, "Okay."

We went on to play the game. I was at the mercy of the audience to guide me, and they didn't let me down. I listened to them, and I won. I was dumbfounded and wondered what was happening. I knew I had just won again, but I didn't know how. It must have been God blessing me, and I was thankful.

When it was time to spin the wheel to see who would be going to the showcase, I spun a seventy-five after two spins. I was pretty sure the next two contestants would knock me out of the running. That didn't happen, and I stood dumbfounded again.

I was going to the showcase. I had no expectations of winning, but I had made it this far and was happy. Winning the showcase was a million to one chance.

I was the first to bid, which meant I could bid or pass it to the other lady. I watched intently as they brought out a piece of jewelry and described it. I thought it might be worth one thousand dollars.

The next item in the showcase was an all-inclusive trip for two to the Cayman Islands. I really liked this because I had never been out of the United States. As a matter of fact, I had never been on a vacation outside of visiting family. So, I had no clue how much a trip like that would cost. I guessed six thousand dollars.

The next item was a brand-new Mitsubishi Lancer, and the audience went wild. I really didn't want a car since I had bought one three months earlier, but I figured if I won it, and that was a big IF in my mind, I could sell it. How much was this car worth? I knew how much my car cost, so I took that into consideration.

I decided to bid on this showcase because I wanted the trip. I looked at my friends in the audience for guidance and could not see them because of all the cameras blocking my view. I figured I came this far with the Holy Spirit guiding me, so I told Drew, "I'll bid $29,000."

I was so glad I chose the first showcase because the next showcase had a tiny sailboat and a trip to Cape Cod.

My opponent must have thought I had overbid because she bid $25,000. I thought she had underbid by a lot.

During the commercial break, we were told that if we won our showcase, we should run toward our prize and not wait.

It was time to reveal the actual price. Drew pulled the card out and said, "Debbie, you bid $29,000 and your actual retail price is $32,732, a difference of $3,732." I thought, that's not bad. At least I didn't go over. Drew walked over to my opponent and pulled her card. He said, "You bid $25,000 and your actual retail price is $33,391, a difference of $8,391." Drew turned to me, shook my hand, and said, "Congratulations!"

I was shocked. I stood there like a dummy in awe of what just happened. The crew on the set were waving me to run. I finally realized I needed to head towards my new car. It was surreal. My friends were told during the commercial break that if I won, they were to leave their seats and join me on stage. Before going off air, Drew came over to congratulate me again. My friends and I were jumping around hugging each other, laughing, hugging the models, and waving at the camera.

If you ever thought game shows were not real, I am here to tell you they are very real. The whole time I was winning, I kept thinking, why me, and thanked God for the blessings He was bestowing on me. Not for one minute did I feel like I was doing any of it on my own. I received all God had planned for me that day, and I was humbled by the experience.

Now for the rest of the story. My husband, Jack, and I had been married thirty-seven years at that point. We never got a real honeymoon, and on our thirty-eighth wedding anniversary, we were on the Cayman Islands celebrating our long-awaited honeymoon. This was God's special gift to us, because two and a half years later Jack went to be with the Lord.

Our God is in the details. One of the sweetest blessings God ever gave me was our honeymoon.

Chapter 10

Peace I leave with you; my peace I give you.
I do not give to you as the world gives.
Do not let your hearts be troubled and do not be afraid.
(JOHN 14:27)

Servant

Every year I pray for a word from God. Every year God gives me one. I love it when the words feel warm and fuzzy like "trust," "victorious," "presence."

God always reveals my word around October or November for the following year. This year, I clearly heard the word "servant." I reminded God that I don't serve well because of my childhood abuse. But He said "servant."

I started thinking about what God could be asking me to do. Am I going to have to clean the church bathrooms? Was God going to send me to Africa? I couldn't begin to understand what it meant or would entail. However, that was the word He had given me, so I wrote it down and waited to see where it would lead me.

I didn't have to wait until the New Year to begin realizing what the road ahead might look like. On December 11,

2017, Jack received a diagnosis of stage four, inoperable lung cancer.

With a heavy heart, I called my daughters in Alaska, and they immediately made plans to come home for Christmas. Even though I was praying for a miracle, I had to face the fact that if Jack didn't get that miracle, this would probably be our last Christmas together.

Jack went into denial and got upset with everybody for making a big fuss. He grumbled that cancer was not a death sentence in the twenty-first century. Even though he insisted nobody come home, they all came.

There were more tests and scans to see if the cancer was anywhere else in his body. On December 29, we were told the cancer was everywhere. He had lung cancer, renal cancer, kidney cancer, and bone cancer. It was as bad as it could get.

I was honored to serve Jack during his battle with cancer and did all I could to make this journey as easy as possible.

I continued to pray for a miracle and trusted God with the outcome. I leaned hard on God for wisdom and strength. I sought His peace daily and did nothing in my own strength because I could so easily fall apart. I clung to Jesus and crawled onto Papa God's lap when I needed a hug and reassurance. I tried not to allow fear to overtake me. Instead, I remembered love, for love casts out fear.

Jack and I had been together forty-five years and married forty of those years. We had raised a family, bought a home, and worked hard. There were difficult times and good times. We even had grandchildren. We had grown old together. As the end of our journey together neared, we could say, "For better or worse, for richer or poorer, in sickness and in health, till death do us part … we kept our vows."

Jack became weaker each day as January rolled around. It was an emotional start to the new year with the dreaded "cancer" word ringing in our ears.

Many thoughts ran through my mind: I know my God. I know He loves us. He can do miracles. I also know our days are numbered. Jack has the promise of eternal life through Jesus, so I know Jack will live and not die. But I want him to get healthy and stay a little longer.

I continued to pray and ask for the cancer to be removed by God's mighty hand. My trust in God never wavered. I rejoiced that He was walking through this valley with us, and I did my best to focus on Jesus and not on the cancer. The entire time, I watched, waited, and continued to serve Jack as we went through this process. I never doubted God and found rest in His presence.

Of course, work didn't stop, so I continued at my job. The time it took to commute to and from work, I conversed with God.

In early January, God gave me a vision, and the meaning was comforting.

In the beginning of our lives, we are confined, secure, and comfortable in a womb. Then we go through the painful process of birth. Once we are born, we are not so confined because now we are in the wide-open world. We have been given life and family. We live through good times and bad times, and we love being alive. However, we're still confined by space and time. When we die, it is painful again as we go through the birthing-of-death process, and then we are in heaven. At that point, we're no longer confined by space and time because heaven doesn't have that. It is more beautiful than we can imagine. There is no more pain. There are no more tears. It's an amazing gift to be eternally in the presence of God.

Jack still took care of himself while I continued to work my full shift. If he had a doctor's appointment, I would stay home and take him.

By February, he was complaining that coffee didn't taste good, and he wasn't eating well. He said his stomach hurt. However, he still got up every day and pet the dogs and enjoyed our little granddaughter, Iris, playing around him. But it was evident that he was becoming more unsteady.

On February 4, he fell for the first time. It scared me so badly. I continued to remind myself that God can do more than I could ever ask or imagine. I refused to lose hope. Huge mountains loomed before us, and I wondered how we would scale their heights.

The answer was clear. I needed to keep my eyes on the path in front of me and on the present journey. I didn't know what was going to happen today or tomorrow, but I needed to trust God. All I could do was lean on the Lord. Our battle with cancer was out of our control.

For I am the LORD your God who takes hold of your right
hand and says to you, Do not fear; I will help you.
(ISAIAH 41:13)

Life continued. I had to go to the Department of Motor Vehicles to get a handicap placard. In the middle of all this, I got a jury summons and had to report to the courts. Jack was in and out of doctor appointments and tests. The car needed it's 90,000-mile maintenance. Amidst all these responsibilities, I still worked.

It was becoming more and more difficult for Jack to get in and out of our high pedestal bed, so I got him a stepstool. Every day seemed to bring new challenges.

It was about this time the doctor suggested chemotherapy and scheduled Jack to be admitted for surgical placement of the chemo port. The hospital scheduled us to take educational sessions for chemo patients and their caregivers.

During these sessions, they educated us and helped us to understand some of the side effects we could expect from chemotherapy. What it sounded like to me was torture. It seemed my husband would live the rest of his days in misery. My heart ached, and I was scared. Jack looked sad and hopeless.

By the time we finished the class, I was convinced I didn't want him to suffer through chemotherapy. When we got home, I told Jack that the chemo scared me more than the cancer. He agreed, so chemo was off the table, and we never went to his appointment.

During February, our daughter Jacquee started researching RSO (Rick Simon Oil) and how they had some really good results with curing cancer. In early February, I called my "Road Dawg" and asked if she would go on a road trip to Oregon to get some RSO for Jack. She was down for the adventure, and we took off from Southern California.

On February 21, Jack started using the RSO. At his next appointment, the doctor noticed his blood test showed his kidneys were improving. Jack's appetite improved also, and he was eating again.

Unfortunately, by the end of February he wasn't eating any longer. We overheard him on the phone saying his stomach hurt all the time. It was time to start thinking about taking leave from work to stay home with him.

Each day when I made my forty-minute drive to and from work, I cried out to God to give us a miracle. I know we are all appointed a time to live and a time to die, but who is ever ready to face the death of a loved one?

A time to be born and a time to die...
(ECCLESIASTES 3:2)

The vows we made to each other over forty years ago, "till death do us part," were ringing true. Death would part us. After all the difficulties of life—marriage, kids, and finances—it appeared that death would separate us until it was my time to die. Only God knew when that would be.

I heard a song, "Even If," by MercyMe, and it became my anthem through the last three months of our life together. The words ministered to me every day. It was as if God was saying to me, "You need to receive My peace and know I am with you."

I felt as though we were sitting on a ticking time bomb. Could we defuse it, or would it explode?

As I watched my husband struggle, a question burned in my heart. Why does my faith waver? Not my faith in God but faith in what God will do or allow. I hated the anticipation of healing or death.

Grief, beautiful grief,
Grief, awful grief,
To grieve means you loved.
Grief, beautiful grief,
Grief, awful grief,
Jesus grieved, and I will too.
Everybody grieves at one time or another.
We all grieve.
Grief is painful.
Anticipated grief is painful.
I thank God for grief.
It shows we care.
It shows we love.
It shows we have feelings.
God-given feelings.
Grief, beautiful grief!
Grief, awful grief!
~ Debbie Powers

I was consumed with Jack's condition. It was all I could think about. One morning on my way to work, I had a conversation with Jesus.

Jesus: Remember, I got this.

Me: I know, Lord, but it's hard to watch.

Jesus: I understand.

Me: Is he going to die?

Jesus: Yes.

Me: Is it going to be dying to self, or is it going to be dying physically?

Jesus: You don't need to know. All you need to know is, I am doing something in him, and it is good. Trust Me.

Me: I do trust You, Lord.

Jesus: You know I love him?

Me: Yes, I know that.

Jesus: I love You, too.

Me: I know. I love you.

Jesus: I am not going to leave either of You alone.

Me: Thank You, Jesus. Thank You for Your presence.

This conversation was as real as if Jesus was right there in the car with me. He comforted me, but I was still very consumed with all the emotions. There were many times I cried out to Him. As I did, He strengthened me to accomplish what I needed to for that day.

The day came when Jack asked if I would help him wash his hair. Another turning point on this journey. Jack didn't like to be served, and it had to be very humbling to ask me to do this for him. Again, I was honored to serve him in this way. Two days later, I helped him take a shower. That was when I noticed how skinny he had become. I wanted to cry. He was a skeleton.

There were days where it was so hard to watch. I reminded myself that it must be even harder to go through all of this as Jack was doing.

One morning he asked me to lay beside him. I crawled into the bed, and he cuddled with me. It was so nice. I wished I would have stayed longer in that moment.

A couple of days later his voice got raspy, and he couldn't speak very loudly. His cough seemed to be labored. He stopped talking unless he needed to say something.

We cooked, and sometimes he ate and sometimes he didn't. We made him tea with electrolyte water, and he had several cups. He looked better.

It had been about three weeks since he started using the RSO. It seemed like a roller coaster ride. Good days and bad days. My emotions were all over the place. One day he seemed to be getting better and the next he seemed to be dying.

It was time for me to go on leave from work. I just couldn't do it anymore, and Jack needed me.

My first day of leave was March 13. I left work and arrived home around 11:45 a.m. Jack was still in bed. He always got up, but not this day. I found him sleeping, and that scared me. I finally got him up and made him some oatmeal. He struggled to eat, but he finally did.

Being home with Jack was helping. He ate, and he looked better. Of course, I made sure he took the RSO three times a day. We were aggressive with it, and it seemed to help.

"Lord, I don't need to know what the future holds, because You hold the future. My hope is You. My trust is in You. No matter what, You got this. You got me. You will strengthen me for the journey ahead. Jack's days are in Your hands. Thank You that You never leave us. I know we could not do this without You. Have mercy, Lord."

Jack's sister, Maggie, and brother, Tom, came from Hawaii. Tom stayed for about a week and then left. Maggie, who happens to be a retired hospice registered nurse, stayed for another week or so. During the time of his family's visit, Jack's closest friends came and spent the day with him. It was hard for his friends to see Jack so sick, but they loved on him, and he really enjoyed their visit.

Maggie bought Jack arthritis pain relief gel tabs and some acid reducer tablets. Two hours after taking them, Jack said, "I feel amazingly good!" He even ate dinner. I loved the little victories we got every now and then.

It wasn't long before Jack asked me to get him a cane. His hip was becoming weaker, and he had difficulty putting weight on it. I found my dad's old cane, and Jack started using it.

There was another concern. We were running out of RSO. I was able to send money and had a friend deliver my order to me in Las Vegas. I drove to Vegas and back in one day, and we didn't run out of the oil.

Several days later, Jack had a doctor's appointment, but he couldn't walk. I had to wheel him in a wheelchair. He hadn't been eating again. The doctor said Jack had thrush, and that was what was causing his stomach to hurt so badly. He gave him two medicines, one for the thrush and one for stomach acid. The doctor prescribed a walker with a seat, and we went to the medical supply place to pick it up. His doctor referred him to the radiation oncologist to get radiation on Jack's bone cancer in his hip.

By the end of March, Jack started getting confused about little things. His body had become so weak that he had trouble walking and getting up from the couch. He had no strength to get out of bed, even though he tried.

It was hard seeing him suffer. I couldn't sleep well. The impending grief was tearing me apart. I could literally see Jack slipping away.

I knew God could turn this all around, even at this stage of the journey. I cried out for healing and mercy.

There was a running debate in my head about how to care for Jack. I didn't know if there was a right way and a wrong way. I questioned myself all the time. Do I make him eat? Do I make him get out of bed? Do I leave him alone and just make sure he is comfortable?

Desperate for answers, I went to the City of Hope to talk to somebody who might have some answers. They informed me there was no right way or wrong way. They didn't give me any kind of guidance; just told me it was whatever we wanted. Then they asked if I wanted hospice care. Everything within me resisted the suggestion because I knew what it meant. I didn't want to accept that my husband was now at the end.

Exhaling a frustrated breath, I said, "Yes."

I was scared and began to hover over him. I was especially afraid he'd fall. I asked him to call me if he needed to get up, but he never would. He became frustrated with me because I wouldn't leave him alone.

Early one morning I heard him get up. I jumped to help him. He refused my assistance, so I stood close by. When he tried to get back into bed, he fell backwards. Good thing I was there to catch him. I let him down slowly and then got my daughter to help me get him into bed.

ProCare Hospice came and did the admissions paperwork. The nurse ordered some liquid medicine for the thrush because the doctor's order was pills, and Jack couldn't take them. However, Jack was uncooperative about taking the medicine. I threatened to put him in the hospital, so he finally took it.

He kept asking for food, but when we brought it to him, he didn't eat. He wanted to but couldn't. I started keeping track of when he took his medicine, when he went to the bathroom, and when he ate and how much.

Pretty soon he was staying in bed and only getting up to go to the bathroom. He still refused to let me help him. When he got up, I would hear the walker and jump to help him. So, he stopped using the walker. His hip became so weak that he was unable to put any weight on it, but he continued to push himself. He waited until I wasn't around and then tried to go by himself. While I was talking to the hospice nurse in the living room, Jack fell and was unable to get up. We had to help him back on his feet. Later that day, my brother happened to see him trying again and ran just in time to catch him before he fell.

Although sad, scared, and tired, I managed. But I didn't handle anger well, and I got mad. I understood that Jack was trying to hold on to his dignity. I got that. But his stubbornness was making me a nervous wreck. After getting out of bed and falling twice in one day, I ordered the hospital bed. It arrived the next day.

I had to make room for the hospital bed and started clearing out and cleaning up an area in our room. Jack asked me what I was doing. Since I was mad, I said, "None of your business. Don't worry about it." I am pretty sure he figured it out because he started cooperating.

The hospital bed would make it safer for him. Our bed was too high, and it was dangerous in his condition. He wouldn't be happy about it, but it was about his safety.

"Servant" took on a whole new meaning for me. Jack was never dependent on me. As a matter of fact, he would scold me if I tried waiting on him. He just wasn't that guy. He did his own laundry. He made his own coffee. He even cooked. When we first got together and I cooked, he told me I didn't know how. Being the brat that I was, I told him I liked his cooking better, and he could cook for me the rest of my life.

To serve him was humbling for both of us. I read a book by Sandra Weinberg, called *#HospiceIsAGift*, and in it she said:

> You have to be comfortable with death. You must find ways of celebrating life in the midst of death and dying. It is necessary for us to

understand the beauty that "a good death" can bring.

When this world has nothing of value left to sell, pitch, or promote, hearts become free to receive gifts that have always been extended but were perhaps neglected or unrecognized before. The labor of love to care for one who is unable to care for themselves is intense.

We are created for wholeness with the capacity to cradle both joy and sorrow in our arms, tending to each as we would an infant.[1]

Jack was becoming even more confused and weak. He was still sitting up several times a day but only for a few minutes at best. One night he reached out while I was asleep and patted me. I jumped awake and asked him what was wrong. He said, "I thought you were the dog."

It became obvious that his time was near. When would be the right time to call our kids to come home?

I prayed, "Lord, comfort us as we prepare to say goodbye. This journey has been hard, and we could not have done it without You. Thank You for all the moments in life that made up our story. It was a life together. Doing it wrong many times but getting it right many times, too. Thank You for our marriage and our family. Thank You for the things we taught each other. Thank You for Jack's strength and integrity to work hard and provide for our family. Thank You that

---

1   Rev. Sandra Weinberg, *#HospiceIsAGift*, (Boise: WIPublish, 2018), 78.

we learned to accept each other's opinions and respect each other's views. Thank You that I got to serve him in his last days on earth. Let his homegoing be a beautiful experience for him and all of us that get the privilege to witness it. My heart is sad, and I don't know how to do this, so thank You for never leaving me and helping us through this process. It hurts so bad. The pain is too deep, but we must keep moving on to our destination. Thank You, Jesus, for walking with us through this storm."

The hospice nurse came by and took his vitals. She reported that they were strong and good. However, he was very dehydrated, and it was causing his confusion, weakness, and lethargy.

Several healthcare personnel visited daily, and my nurse told me they were all amazed that Jack wasn't in pain. She explained to me that bone cancer patients are usually in extreme pain, and hospice would have to go out to homes two and three times a day to try and regulate their pain medication.

I explained to her that Jack had a high pain tolerance, and he would not always let you know he was in pain.

She told me she would know if he was in discomfort because his blood pressure would be elevated, but his was normal.

I was blessed that my sister-in-law, Maggie, was arriving again from Hawaii to help me.

When Maggie arrived, we tag-teamed waking up every hour and making him sip water. He did well, and by morning he seemed to be doing better.

My youngest daughter, Jacquee, wanted to talk to her Aunt Maggie. Unfortunately, Maggie was here to help Jack die, and Jacquee and the rest of us were still holding onto hope.

We weren't dealing with just the cancer now. We were dealing with thrush and dehydration too. Through all this, Jack asked when he was going to see the oncologist again. I don't think I answered him because I knew he wouldn't.

The bone cancer began to cause pain in his ribs, so Maggie gave him a small dose of morphine to ease his discomfort. This made me fearful because once the morphine started, the end was near.

> *Be strong and courageous. Do not be afraid or terrified,*
> *for the LORD your God goes with you;*
> *he will never leave you nor forsake you.*
> (DEUTERONOMY 31:6)

Maggie was a big help, and I thanked God she was with me. She was my helper and my teacher. The hardest part about having her assist me was that she was real with me. I didn't want real. I wanted a miracle.

I was sad on so many levels. At the same time, I felt blessed to have been married to Jack for forty years. I even felt blessed to be able to do this hard thing that God had called me to. I was blessed that God always provides. I was blessed to have loved and been loved.

Early one morning, Jack was very alert and had no pain. He sat up in bed and let me shave him and take his picture. He looked so good and even talked a little. He had four bites of scrambled eggs and two bites of oatmeal. He even drank water regularly.

His friends, Joe and Neil, came back to visit. These men loved each other like brothers. They hung out around his hospital bed and watched TV with him. Jack wasn't talking much because of the thrush, but I could see how much he appreciated the boys coming to visit. These are the guys he grew up with. They went to school together, got in trouble together, and stayed friends for sixty years or more. Not many people could say that.

A day or two later Jack was confused again. He tried to talk but his voice was pretty much gone, and I couldn't understand him. This frustrated him and made him mad to the point that he cursed at Maggie and me and said he was going to hit us. Maggie told me this could go on for months or turn overnight.

I decided it was time to get the kids home. I called each of them, and they made arrangements to fly home.

The RSO was a blessing even if it didn't take the cancer away. It did so many other amazing things for Jack. Maggie said the RSO kept him from constipation, which usually is very unpleasant at this stage of dying. He had not experienced the unbearable pain that comes with cancer and the unimaginable pain that comes with bone cancer.

Maggie continued to keep it real with me and told me it was going to get worse. As we continued through the process, there would be new hurdles.

My emotions were all over the place. It was so hard.

A nurse was able to get an IV into his hand. This brought all kinds of new challenges. He kept trying to remove it, and we had to always stay with him. Confusion was a daily thing now. Jack was so determined to pull the IV out that I snapped at him, "You need this. It is giving you fluids. Without fluids you will die! Do you want to die?"

"Yes," he answered.

Oh, Lord, I need to let him go.

I explained to Jack that I was going to send for our daughters and then he could go. I assured him we would be okay.

My tears flowed freely. I wouldn't wish this on anybody.

To keep Jack calm, I slept in the hospital bed with him hoping this would hinder him from pulling his IV out in his sleep. It worked. The IV was still in place in the morning. Maggie had changed the bag of fluids in the middle of the night without any issue.

> *Love never gives up, never loses faith, is always hopeful,*
> *and endures through every circumstance.*
> (1 CORINTHIANS 13:7)

Jack slept all day now. He hardly drank any water. He finished the last bag of fluids, and hospice told us that another bag would do no good. We set up the oxygen just in case we needed it.

He was truly dying. My daughters were on their way, and I prayed they would make it home before he passed. He was very out of it, but the nurse told me his vitals were still good.

Jack opened his eyes every once in a while and messed with his blanket or his catheter. It was obvious he wasn't quite there. He was alive, but he wasn't. I wanted to think it was that peaceful moment right before the Lord came for him. It was strange to witness and heartbreaking at the same time.

"Lord, help me. I'm not being very gracious or kind in my spirit. People give advice or input, and it hits me the wrong way. It's not that the advice or input isn't good. I just don't want to hear it. I'm trying to keep a sweet spirit about me, but sometimes I feel I'm faking it. How am I supposed to act as a child of God? I'm not the only one grieving here. Yet I'm sitting here feeling sorry for myself. I wonder why it must be like this. How much more will we have to endure?

"Is Jack aware of what is happening to him? Is he having conversations with You, Lord?

"Help me be strong, kind, and understanding. It's hard to face another day watching him slip away from us. Forgive me for using foul language when I've been frustrated, had unkind thoughts, when my heart wasn't right, when I forgot to trust You, and when I felt sorry for myself. Forgive me, Lord."

It was only two weeks ago when Jack was still getting out of bed and sitting in the living room. It seemed like it had been months since he interacted with us, yet it had only been two weeks.

Then Jack really hurt himself. He pulled on his catheter in the middle of the night, which made his bladder spasm. He was in excruciating pain, and because of his confused state of mind, he wanted to pull on it again.

Maggie and I held his hands through the night. I got on one side of him in the hospital bed and Maggie slept on our bed, on the other side of him. We gave him two small doses of morphine and a half of an anxiety pill. Nothing was working. Through this whole process, I never saw him wrench in pain the way he did when the bladder spasmed. The spasms would last about ten seconds, and we would hold on to his hands real tight until it passed.

There was a little book, *The Dying Experience*, that the hospice nurse gave me. It helped me to understand what Jack was going through and how it was part of the progression to the other side. It helped me to stop freaking out every time he did something that scared me. I felt blessed that she had given it to me to read.

My youngest daughter, Jacquee, and her husband, Buddy, got on their standby flight and were arriving on Thursday morning. Jessie also got on a flight and was arriving Thursday afternoon. Maggie's daughter, Maria, was coming in on Thursday evening. Nikki lived with us, so she was home.

Thursday was the hardest day so far. Jack was in pain all day from the bladder spasms. We finally gave him some more morphine and anxiety medicine. When that didn't work, we kicked it up and gave him more. He finally settled down and was resting well. Even though he was pretty much out of it, we all rallied around him and loved on him. Maria even sang to him. It was hard to see my daughters' hearts breaking as they held Jack's hand and kissed him.

I was so glad that all our daughters were at his bedside. They all made it in time. It was God's grace and mercy.

On Friday morning, I got up to go to the bathroom around 6:00 a.m. Jack was still breathing. I laid back down and held his hand. At around 6:25 I heard my brother using the bathroom. Maggie looked up and noticed Jack was still breathing and moved his hand a little.

Then I heard my brother let the dogs in about three minutes later. I looked over at Jack. He wasn't breathing. I waited to see if he would start breathing again because that was what he had been doing throughout the night. When I didn't see him take another breath, I pulled back the covers to check if his heart was beating. He was so thin that I had been able see his heart beating in his stomach. There was no heartbeat. I put my ear to his chest. Nothing.

I woke Maggie up and told her I thought Jack was gone. She checked him, and he was indeed gone.

It was a beautiful sunny spring morning. Sunshine streamed through the window. Jack had gone peacefully, and he was in the arms of Jesus.

Maggie cleaned him up and removed the catheter while I went to wake up my daughters to let them know their dad was gone. Gratefulness filled my heart that our girls had made it home just the day before.

I didn't know if Jack had willed himself to stay alive or if, in God's mercy, He allowed Jack to stay alive until his children made it home. Either way, I was thankful.

We all gathered around his bed. Maria put rose pedals over his sheet and sang "Amazing Grace."

Jack's journey on earth was over, but his journey in eternity had just begun. It was time for me to learn how to do life without my Jack, my love. God had been so gracious to me. Maggie had been with me to help during the last week of Jack's life. The kids made it home just in time. Jesus never left my side. He held me through all the ups and downs.

Jack and I always said we would donate our bodies to science, so that was what I did. Research for Life came and did a beautiful job removing him from our home. Because he was an Army veteran, they draped him with the American flag. We walked him out with Jacquee and me on his right side and Nikki and Jessie on his left side. Maggie was at his feet.

It was hard to believe he was gone. What a legacy he left to his children. He wasn't a perfect man, but he was a good man. I was blessed to be able to say I was his wife.

The next day we held a Celebration of Life at our home. His friends, cousins, coworkers, and neighbors dropped their plans and came to honor this hardworking family man at a moment's notice. They helped our family celebrate our beloved Jack. God again gave us favor.

With everybody pitching in, we had food, pictures, a memorial flyer, and a slide show. People brought so many flowers that our home smelled like spring. It was beautiful.

He would truly be missed.

Chapter 11

Take delight in the Lord, and he will give you
the desires of your heart.
(Psalm 37: 4)

The Bucket List

Many people have bucket lists. I never had one. At least I didn't think I did until I was in my sixties. That was when I realized I had one after all.

It wasn't written on paper. Instead, it existed in my mind. As I thought back on my life, I saw it. Even as a little girl, I wanted to be a wife and mommy. More than that, I wanted to have a healthy family—something I didn't have growing up. By God's grace I was blessed with all three. It wasn't perfect, but who has perfect?

Another thing I remember wanting as a child was to be on two game shows. Living in the Los Angeles area, I had easy access to both studios where they were filmed. As I mentioned in one of my previous stories, I was able to realize that dream.

Another game show fell into my lap. I don't remember how I found out about it, but this one was *The Perfect Match*, and my husband would have to be a part of the interview process.

Jack was not *that* guy, and to this day I don't know how I convinced him to audition. I remember him telling me, if I ended up getting him on national TV, he would never forgive me. Well, *I* didn't get us on that show. But Jack was so funny that they fell in love with him, and *he* got us on the show. We ended up being the winning couple.

Not very many people will remember *The Perfect Match* because it only lasted one season.

Another thing on the bucket list that I didn't know existed was that I wanted to be a homeowner. As a young mother and wife, I didn't think it was possible. We worked hard but lived paycheck to paycheck. Then it happened. The home we bought was beautiful. Truth be told, it was in the middle of nowhere, but it was ours. We raised our children and grew old in our home.

TV and movies left an impression on me from a young age. I dreamed of being an actress someday. In my thirties, I landed my first play in a small local theater. Then I went on to do more little theaters. As I grew close to the Lord, I became involved in church productions—directing plays, writing skits, and performing. I lovingly became the "Drama Queen" to my church family. That's not necessarily a name you want pinned on yourself, but I wore the title proudly around my brothers and sisters in Christ.

A big part of my bucket list was about acting. I always thought it would be fun to be in a commercial or movie.

Well, there's a lot that goes into that, and there are a lot of scams out there that will take your money and promise you the world. Also, there was the union. You can't get into the union without having worked, and you can't work without being in the union. There were ways to get around this dilemma, but you had to know how.

At some point I figured I could maybe do background/extra work. The good thing about that would be, no lines to memorize and it was easy work. You don't make a lot of money, but you could be part of a movie, music video, or commercial. To me, that would be a lot of fun.

I decided that one day I would seriously look into this. One day ... after I retired, because you can't work full time and be available to do gigs at the drop of a hat. This would be the perfect retirement adventure for me.

For the first two years of retirement, I didn't think about my bucket list. Then one day I made up my mind to look for a part-time job, but nothing I saw appealed to me. I had worked for over forty-five years and didn't want to get sucked back into the grind of corporate America.

Out of nowhere—although I'm sure it was the Holy Spirit—I remembered I wanted to do extra work in a movie. I pulled out my laptop and started researching so I wouldn't get scammed. I found that there were casting call websites, and I researched all the top ones. I decided to investigate the top-rated one.

Ouch! It cost two hundred dollars a year for the subscription. I didn't want to spend that much on something that wasn't a sure thing. I had no guarantee I could get any work, so I prayed about it. I went back and read, pondered, and prayed some more for the next several days.

I must be clear about something here. Getting scammed wouldn't entail a couple of hundred dollars. It would entail thousands. And they promised photos, an agent, and guaranteed work.

These casting websites don't do this. They offer a subscription, kind of like a magazine, to give you access to projects that are looking for talent. Think of it as a help wanted ad. It's up to you to check the casting calls daily and respond. The way it works is, you make a profile, much like the one on any social media platform. Once you make your profile, you can filter what you want to see. When you respond that you are interested in a project, you will wait to see if the casting director is interested in you. So, it's a lot like answering a help wanted ad.

Back to my pondering and praying. I opened my computer again, and this time I got a pop-up saying that I could sign up for only one hundred dollars for the first year.

Wow! Now that seemed reasonable to me. I was willing to gamble one hundred dollars. Plus, since I had been praying about it, I figured it was God giving me the go ahead.

I bit the bullet, paid the subscription fee, and set up my profile. I filtered my age, gender, and a few other categories and applied for a few projects. Within two days, I got hired. They called an online meeting with all the talent they had chosen. Now this is where I knew God was in it. The first thing they said was, "The name of the movie is *At the Cross*, and we will be filming in a church."

Okay, God, I hear You loud and clear.

And you know what? It paid one hundred dollars.

Life is a journey. Enjoy it.

Chapter 12

Midwifery

L iving in the middle of nowhere meant that when I went
to town, I always did as much as I could before return-
ing home. On my comfortable thirty-minute drive back to
my house, I stopped at Walmart to pick up a few items. I
enjoyed shopping by myself because I didn't feel rushed and
could shop at my leisure. I grabbed a cart, and pulled up to
the sanitizing wipes to wipe the grocery cart before continu-
ing into the store. Since I faced the exit doors, I had to back
up to turn around. In the process, I bumped into a young lady
standing right behind me. Horrified, I apologized profusely.

The young lady pushed me and yelled, "Hey, watch where
you're going!"

"I didn't see you there. I'm sorry. I didn't mean to bump
into you."

"Yes, you did. Look at all this room." She waved her arms in a sweeping gesture to show how much room I had. Pushing me again, she yelled, "You ran into me on purpose!"

I reached out to gently touch her shoulder in a conciliatory manner, and said, "I'm so sorry. I didn't do it on purpose."

She aggressively shrugged off my hand.

I felt uncomfortable but not scared. Was anybody witnessing this craziness?

At that moment, another young lady about five feet away pointed her cell phone at me as she stared me down. I shrugged my shoulders as if to say, "I don't know what just happened."

I noticed a young man coming up behind us pushing a cart. He watched us. I gave him a look like this girl is crazy. All the while this lady continued in her attempt to provoke me.

I am not a confrontational person, so I slowly pushed my cart into the store after I apologized a few more times.

I was upset. No, I was mad. It added fuel to the fire burning inside me when I saw all three of them shopping together in the store. I wanted to confront them and ask what that was all about, but I didn't. I thought about reporting the incident to the store management, but I didn't. It was impossible to shop. My blood boiled. I kept asking God, "Why did that happen? I'm angry, and I don't like feeling this way."

My thoughts were cycling, and I was letting my emotions get the best of me. I needed to leave, to get in a safe place.

I left the store, got into my car, and started home—alone with God. I was so angry, I cried. Hateful feelings coursed through me, and I asked God to please take these horrible emotions away.

The conversation was one-sided until I asked Him what His purpose was in that whole unpleasant incident. He said, "I love her as much as I love you."

Ah, man. "Yes, I know, Lord. But I still don't know why I had to encounter her."

"I want you to pray for her. Pray for her salvation," He gently explained.

Immediately peace returned. I wasn't angry anymore. My heart overflowed with love for that angry young lady. Not only did I pray for her right there in my car on my drive home, but I also shared this story with our women's ministry, and we all began praying for her. My prayers for that young lady continued for probably six months or more.

I never saw her again. If I had, I don't think I would have recognized her.

God had a purpose. I needed to calm down so He could reveal it to me.

One day, I chatted with a friend who works at a Walmart, and she told me that there are people who do this kind of stuff hoping to get into a fight. A second person will video-tape the whole thing, and then they sue the store because it happened on their property.

I thank God I wasn't confrontational. Could you imagine if I had confronted her? God's grace.

After sharing this story over the years, I recently had a lovely sister in the Lord tell me she envisioned a midwife delivering a baby.

Midwifery is the profession or practice of assisting in childbirth. What a beautiful picture of helping to deliver the unsaved out of darkness through our prayers.

Chapter 13

*Trust in the L*ORD *with all your heart;*
do not depend on your own understanding.
Seek his will in all you do,
and he will show you which path to take.
(PROVERBS 3:5–6)

Body Shop

I drove my ten-year-old car to the body shop to see if I could afford to make it look new again. My heart's desire was a new car, but that wasn't in the budget. Living on Social Security, things were tight and there was no way I could qualify for a new car loan. I decided if the repairs were under one thousand dollars, I would get it done.

I researched all the body shops in my area and chose the one with the highest customer satisfaction rating. The gentleman was very polite. He did the inspection and wrote up an estimate that was under one thousand dollars. He informed me that he would need the vehicle for two days. I agreed to call him back on Friday to set up an appointment for the following Tuesday.

On my way home, I stopped to pick up a few items at the store. As I was pulling out to continue home, my car made a horrible noise, jolted, and the engine light came on. The noise stopped as suddenly as it had started. However, there was no way I was going to drive home and possibly get stranded on the side of the road in the middle of the desert. If it stopped running, that was exactly where I would be.

I turned around and went straight to my mechanic. After waiting for two hours for the diagnostics to be run, the news was not good. I needed a new engine, which would cost ten thousand dollars. Yikes!

My vehicle had 181,000 miles on it. I had faithfully done the maintenance every five thousand miles. I couldn't believe the engine was going out.

At the advice of my brother, I took it to the dealership and paid to have them do another diagnostic to get a second opinion. They informed me it could be the head gaskets, which would cost six thousand dollars. However, once they opened the engine, they might find that the engine needed replacing, and that would be thirteen thousand dollars. Double yikes!

I asked how much they would give me for a trade-in. They said they could possibly give me one thousand dollars, but then they didn't know what they would do with the vehicle.

When the news changes from one thousand dollars to do some body work to thirteen thousand dollars for a new engine, you need time to process what to do. Which meant it was time to pray.

I rented a vehicle from the dealership and went home to see how God was going to direct me. I struggled the rest of the day. The little savings that I had could buy a used car, but there was no way of knowing what I might end up with. I also worried about spending my savings, which I was using to supplement my monthly income. Yet I needed a dependable car.

God was quiet as I wrestled with what I was going to do. Since I was reasoning with Him, I thought He would give me a sign of how I should proceed. But after I stopped reasoning for a moment, He gently spoke, "You have the money to buy a new car."

"I do?"

"Yes, in your 401K."

"But Lord, I'm not supposed to touch that. It's for when I'm old."

"Why do you hold on to your worldly possessions with clenched fists? Let go and trust Me to take care of you."

Once I heard that, I felt at peace. Besides, it wasn't like I was going to empty my 401K.

I started researching vehicles, and after two days, I found the one I wanted. I decided not to use my old vehicle as a trade-in. Perhaps, I'd donate it to some charity.

I made an appointment to pick up my new vehicle on Saturday. There was one thing I still pondered. Why had I been led to the body shop if my car was going to breakdown? I questioned the Lord, only because in my experience everything happens for a reason, but He didn't answer. This wasn't the first time I wanted to know why, and God made it clear that I didn't need to know.

On Friday, I felt a gentle nudge to call the body shop and let them know I wouldn't be bringing my car in for repairs. I hadn't planned on calling them back, but the Lord was impressing me to make a courtesy call. When the gentleman answered the phone, he remembered me, and when I told him what had happened and how the dealership said they would give me one thousand dollars for my car, he offered to give me that same amount. He wanted to fix it and give it to his wife as a family car.

After I ended the call, I said to the Lord, "So that was why I had to go to the body shop. I needed to establish a relationship with the man who would buy my car."

God directs our paths. He goes before us. Thank You, Jesus.

Chapter 14

When Jesus had called the Twelve together,
he gave them power and authority to drive out all demons
and to cure diseases.
(Luke 9:1)

For our struggle is not against flesh and blood,
but against the rulers, against the authorities, against the
powers of this dark world and against the spiritual forces of
evil in the heavenly realms.
(Ephesians 6:12)

The weapons we fight with are not the weapons
of the world. On the contrary, they have divine
power to demolish strongholds.
(2 Corinthians 10:4)

Spiritual Warfare

When I got saved, I was on fire for the Lord. I was so hungry to learn everything I could about God. The first five years were an adventure. The more I learned, the more I wanted to learn. I was at church all the time. I wanted to be used by the Lord.

One day the youth pastor asked if I would help by being a driver for "Church on the Beach." I must admit, I was excited about going to the beach.

The morning of the trip, Jacquee, my four-year-old, got sick. She sat on the commode with stomach cramps. This was going to be a problem. I would have to stay home with her, and Pastor would be short a driver.

Then I had a thought. Could this be the enemy trying to keep us from Church on the Beach? Maybe I should lay hands on my daughter and pray for her. But what if it doesn't work? What would Jacquee think if she didn't get well? Would she get confused about the power of God?

I felt a strong impression to lay hands on her, pray, and take authority in the name of Jesus. Still afraid that nothing would happen, I prayed, "Father God, I ask that You heal Jacquee. You said that I can ask anything in Your name, so I am asking in faith. If this is an attack from the enemy, I cancel his assignment in the powerful name of Jesus Christ.

"Satan, you have no power or authority. I plead the blood of Jesus over Jacquee. And Satan, you cannot stand in the presence of the cleansing blood of Christ. So be gone in Jesus's name. Amen."

Jacquee looked up at me and said, "I feel better, Mommy."

I am ashamed to admit that I didn't believe her. I thought she just wanted to go to the beach, and she knew that if she didn't feel better, we weren't going. I was afraid that I was going to drive the two hours to the beach, and then Jacquee would tell me she was feeling sick again, and we'd have to leave.

To my surprise, she really was well. We stayed at the beach all day and had a great time.

That was not the last time Jacquee was under attack by the enemy. The next time was a lot more frightening.

When she was about five years old, she started having terrible nightmares. She would wake up and come running into our bedroom. Her heart beat out of her little chest as she cried and told us that a big, ugly wolf with long, bloody fangs was chasing her. I comforted her and pulled her into bed with us. Unfortunately, this continued night after night.

One day when I was at church, I mentioned the nightmares to a few people. They told me it was a demonic attack, and I needed to do spiritual warfare.

"Spiritual warfare?" I said, "How do I do that?" I was scared for my child. How do you fight the devil?

I got a crash course right there from my brothers and sisters in Christ. They explained that there was an evil presence in my daughter's room, and I needed to pray over her and take authority over this presence in the name of Jesus. They explained that evil must flee when it hears the name of Jesus. They encouraged me by reminding me that I had the Holy Spirit living inside of me, and I was a child of God. This gave me the right and the power to take the authority God gave to me through the Holy Spirit. I would not be doing anything in my power. It would be God's power working through me.

I took what they told me and boldly did what they had said.

That night when I tucked Jacquee into bed, I prayed out loud, "Father, I ask for Your protection over Jacquee as she sleeps tonight. I plead the blood of Jesus over her and her bedroom.

"I speak to any demonic presence and tell you that your assignment is canceled in the mighty name of Jesus. When I speak the name of Jesus, demons must flee. You have no power or authority.

"Lord, place Your angels around this room to watch over and protect Jacquee as she sleeps. I pray all this in Jesus's name. Amen."

When we awoke the next morning, Jacquee had slept through the night for the first time in days. We repeated the prayer each night, and each night Jacquee slept peacefully. After about two weeks, I figured the demonic presence was gone, and I didn't pray the prayer that night.

The demon took that opportunity to return, and Jacquee had another scary nightmare and ran into our room once again with her heart beating out of her chest. For the next two weeks, I faithfully prayed the spiritual warfare prayer as I tucked her into bed. Then I figured it was time to stop again.

I shouldn't have done that because the nightmare returned. Believe it or not, I did this routine again and stopped again. I guess I figured this thing would give up eventually, but I was wrong.

The third time around, Jacquee didn't wake me up, and I thought, okay, it finally left. Except the next morning Jacquee told me, "Mommy, I had another nightmare last night."

"Oh, really? You didn't wake me up."

She said the most wonderful thing. "Nope, I told it to leave in the name of Jesus, and it did."

I hugged her and said how proud I was of her for taking authority over it in Jesus's name. Once she did that, she slept peacefully again, and the demon never returned.

Chapter 15

A soft answer turns away wrath,
But a harsh word stirs up anger.
(Proverbs 15:1 NKJV)

Soft Answer

Living in the world without Christ, we develop some really bad habits. One of those habits is to feel we must argue about anything and everything. During a Bible study with the women's group, we were learning about Proverbs 15:1.

I loved what was being taught. It made sense. These beautiful ladies were mentoring me in the ups and downs of life. I had very few positive influences in my life, and for the first time, I was learning how to be a godly mom and wife. It was empowering. I couldn't wait to apply what I had learned.

Before long, I was able to do just that. While Jack and I were having a conversation, I said something that he took the wrong way. He got very angry.

I remembered my Bible study about a soft answer turning away wrath, and I started backpedaling. I apologized.

"Honey, I didn't mean it like that. I'm sorry. You misunderstood what I was saying. Will you forgive me?"

"No, I will not," was his angry reply. He ranted for several minutes about whatever it was.

"Well, I'm sorry. I didn't mean to make you mad. Obviously, my presence is upsetting you, so I'm going to remove myself and go to our room to get out of your way."

I shut the door to our bedroom, looked up to heaven, and said, "Well, that didn't work."

About five minutes later Jack entered the room. His head hung in shame, and he said, "I'm sorry. I shouldn't have acted that way. Of course, I forgive you."

We hugged, and I realized that a soft answer truly does turn away wrath.

If you enjoyed this book, will you help me spread the word?

There are several ways you can help me get the word out about the message of this book...

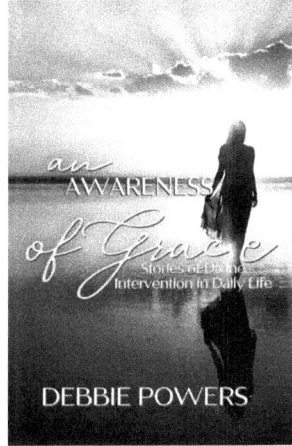

- Post a 5-Star review on Amazon.
- Write about the book on your Facebook, Twitter, Instagram, LinkedIn—any social media you regularly use!
- If you blog, consider referencing the book, or publishing an excerpt from the book with a link back to my website. You have my permission to do this if you provide proper credit and backlinks.
- Recommend the book to friends—word-of-mouth is still the most effective form of advertising.

You can reach me at: www.anawarenessofgrace.com

www.ingramcontent.com/pod-product-compliance
Lightning Source LLC
Chambersburg PA
CBHW072353090426
42741CB00012B/3025